The Giant Raft, Tr. by W.J. Gordon

Jules Verne

THE GIANT RAFT.
(PART I.)
EIGHT HUNDRED LEAGUES ON THE AMAZON.

London:

SAMPSON LOW, MARSTON, SEARLE, AND RIVINGTON,

CROWN BUILDINGS, 188, FLEET STREET.

1881.

THE GIANT RAFT.

(PART I.)

EIGHT HUNDRED LEAGUES ON THE AMAZON.

BY

JULES VERNE.

TRANSLATED BY W. J. GORDON.

London:

SAMPSON LOW, MARSTON, SEARLE, AND RIVINGTON,

CROWN BUILDINGS, 188, FLEET STREET.

1881.

LONDON :
PRINTED BY GILBERT AND RIVINGTON, LIMITED,
ST. JOHN'S SQUARE.

CONTENTS.

LIST OF ILLUSTRATIONS.

THE GIANT RAFT.

CHAPTER I.

A CAPTAIN OF THE WOODS.

"Phyjslyddqfdzxgasgzzqqehxgkfndrxuj
ugiocytdxvksbxhhuypohdvyrymhuhpuydkjo
xphetozsletnpmvffovpdpajxhyynojyggayme
qynfuqlnmvlyfgsuzmqiztlbqgyugsqeubvn
rcredgruzblrmxyuhqhpzdrrgcrohepqxufiv
vrplphonthvddqfhqsntzhhhnfepmqkyuuex
ktogzgkyuumfvijdqdpzjqsykrplxhxqrymvkl
ohhhotozvdksppsuvjhd."

THE man who held in his hand the document of which
this strange assemblage of letters formed the concluding
paragraph, remained for some moments lost in thought.

It contained about a hundred of these lines, with the
letters at even distances, and undivided into words. It
seemed to have been written many years before, and time

had already laid his tawny finger on the sheet of good stout paper which was covered with the hieroglyphics.

On what principle had these letters been arranged? He who held the paper was alone able to tell. With such cipher languages it is as with the locks of some of our iron safes,—in either case the protection is the same. The combinations which they lead to can be counted by millions, and no calculator's life would suffice to express them. Some particular "word" has to be known before the lock of the safe will act, and some "cipher" is necessary before the cryptogram can be read.

He who had just reperused the document was but a simple "captain of the woods." Under the name of "Capitaes do Mato" are known in Brazil those individuals who are engaged in the recapture of fugitive slaves. The institution dates from 1722. At that period anti-slavery ideas had entered the minds of but a few philanthropists, and more than a century had to elapse before the mass of the people grasped and applied them. That freedom was a right, that the very first of the natural rights of man was to be free and to belong only to himself, would seem to be self-evident, and yet thousands of years had to pass before the glorious thought was generally accepted, and the nations of the earth had the courage to proclaim it.

In 1852, the year in which our story opens, there were still slaves in Brazil, and as a natural consequence, captains of the woods to pursue them. For certain reasons of political economy the hour of general emancipation had been delayed, but the black had at this date the right to ransom himself, the children which were born to him were born free. The day was not far distant when the magnificent country, into which could be put three-quarters of the continent of Europe, would no longer count a single slave amongst its ten millions of inhabitants.

The occupation of the captains of the woods was doomed, and at the period we speak of the advantages obtainable from the capture of fugitives were rapidly diminishing. While, however, the calling continued sufficiently profitable, the captains of the woods formed a peculiar class of adventurers, principally composed of freedmen and deserters —of not very enviable reputation. The slave-hunters in fact belonged to the dregs of society, and we shall not be far wrong in assuming that the man with the cryptogram was a fitting comrade for his fellow "capitaes do mato." Torres—for that was his name—unlike the majority of his companions, was neither half-breed, Indian, nor negro. He was a white of Brazilian origin, and had received a better education than befitted his present condition. One of those unclassed men who are found so frequently in the distant countries of the New World, at a time when the Brazilian law still excluded mulattos and others of mixed blood from certain employments, it was evident that if such exclusion had affected him, it had done so on account of his worthless character, and not because of his birth.

Torres at the present moment was not, however, in Brazil. He had just passed the frontier, and was wandering in the forests of Peru, from which issue the waters of the Upper Amazon.

He was a man of about thirty years of age, on whom the fatigues of a precarious existence seemed, thanks to an exceptional temperament and an iron constitution, to have had no effect. Of middle height, broad shoulders, regular features, and decided gait, his face was tanned with the scorching air of the tropics. He had a thick black beard, and eyes lost under contracting eyebrows, giving that swift but hard glance so characteristic of insolent natures. Clothed as backwoodsmen are generally clothed, not over elaborately, his garments bore witness to long and roughish wear. On his head, stuck jauntily on one side, was a leather hat with a large brim. Trousers he had of coarse wool, which were tucked into the tops of the thick heavy boots which formed the most substantial part of his attire, and over all, and hiding all, was a faded yellowish " poncho."

But if Torres was a captain of the woods it was evident that he was not now employed in that capacity, his means of attack and defence being obviously insufficient for any one engaged in the pursuit of the blacks. No fire-arms—

neither gun nor revolver. In his belt only one of those weapons, more sword than hunting-knife, called a "manchetta," and in addition he had an "enchada," which is a s ortof hoe, specially employed in the pursuit of the tatous and agoutis which abound in the forests of the Upper Amazon, where there is generally little to fear from wild beasts.

On the 4th of May, 1852, it happened, then, that our adventurer was deeply absorbed in the reading of the document on which his eyes were fixed, and, accustomed as he was to live in the forests of South America, he was perfectly indifferent to their splendours. Nothing could distract his attention ; neither the constant cry of the howling monkeys, which St. Hilaire has graphically compared to the axe of the woodman as he strikes the branches of the trees, nor the sharp jingle of the rings of the rattlesnake (not an aggressive reptile, it is true, but one of the most venomous); neither the bawling voice of the horned toad, the most hideous of its kind, nor even the solemn and sonorous croak of the bellowing frog, which, though it cannot equal the bull in size, can surpass him in noise.

Torres heard nothing of all these sounds, which form, as it were, the complex voice of the forests of the New World. Reclining at the foot of a magnificent tree, he did not even admire the lofty boughs of that " pao ferro," or iron wood, with its sombre bark, hard as the metal which it replaces in the weapon and utensil of the Indian savage. No: Lost in thought, the captain of the woods turned the curious paper again and again between his fingers. With the cipher, of which he had the secret, he assigned to each letter its true value. He read, he verified the sense of those lines, unintelligible to all but him, and then he smiled—and a most unpleasant smile it was.

Then he murmured some phrases in an undertone which none in the solitude of the Peruvian forests could hear, and which no one, had he been anywhere else would have heard.

"Yes," said he, at length, "here are a hundred lines very neatly written, which, for some one that I know have an importance that is undoubted. That somebody is rich. It is a question of life or death for him, and looked at in every way it will cost him something." And, scrutinizing the paper with greedy eyes, "At a conto[1] only for each word of this last sentence it will amount to a considerable sum, and it is this sentence which fixes the price. It sums up the entire document. It gives their true names to true personages; but before trying to understand it I ought to begin by counting the number of words it contains, and even when this is done its true meaning may be missed."

In saying this Torres began to count mentally.

---

[1] One thousand reis are equal to three francs, and a conto of reis is worth three thousand francs.

"There are fifty-eight words, and that makes fifty-eight contos. With nothing but that one could live in Brazil, in America, wherever one wished, and even live without doing anything! And what would it be, then, if all the words of this document were paid for at the same price? It would be necessary to count by hundreds of contos. Ah! there is quite a fortune here for me to realize if I am not the greatest of duffers!"

It seemed as though the hands of Torres felt the enormous sum, and were already closing over the rolls of gold. Suddenly his thoughts took another turn.

"At length," he cried, " I see land ; and I do not regret the voyage which has led me from the coast of the Atlantic to the Upper Amazon. But this man may quit America and go beyond the seas, and then how can I touch him ? But no! he is there, and if I climb to the top of this tree I can see the roof under which he lives with his family!" Then seizing the paper and shaking it with terrible meaning, " Before to-morrow I will be in his presence ; before to-morrow he will know that his honour and his life are contained in these lines. And when he wishes to see the cipher which permits him to read them, he—well, he will pay for it. He will pay, if I wish it, with all his fortune, as he ought to pay with all his blood! Ah! My worthy comrade, who gave me this cipher, who told me where I could find his old colleague, and the name under which he has been hiding himself for so many years, hardly suspects that he has made my fortune!"

For the last time Torres glanced over the yellow paper, and then, after carefully folding it, put it away into a little copper box which he used for a purse. This box was about as big as a cigar-case, and if what was in it was all Torres possessed he would nowhere have been considered a wealthy man. He had a few of all the coins of the neighbouring States—ten double-condors in gold of the United States of Columbia, worth about a hundred francs; Brazilian reis worth about as much; golden sols of Peru, worth, say, double: some Chilian escudos, worth fifty francs or more, and some smaller coins; but the lot would not amount to more than 500 francs, and Torres would have been somewhat embarrassed had he been asked how or where he had got them. One thing was certain, that for some months, after having suddenly abandoned the trade of the slave-hunter, which he carried on in the province of Para, Torres had ascended the basin of the Amazon, crossed the Brazilian frontier, and come into Peruvian territory. To such a man the necessaries of life were but few; expenses he had none —nothing for his lodging, nothing for his clothes. The forest provided his food, which in the backwoods cost him nought. A few reis were enough for his tobacco, which he bought at the mission-stations or in the villages, and for a trifle more he filled his flask with liquor. With little he could go far.

When he had pushed the paper into the metal box, of which the lid shut tightly with a snap, Torres, instead of putting it into the pocket of his under-vest, thought to be extra careful, and placed it near him in a hollow of a root of the tree beneath which he was sitting. This proceeding as it turned out, might have cost him dear.

It was very warm ; the air was oppressive. If the church of the nearest village had possessed a clock, the clock would have struck two, and, coming with the wind, Torres would have heard it, for it was not more than a couple of miles off. But he cared not as to time. Accustomed to regulate his proceedings by the height of the sun, calculated with more or less accuracy, he could scarcely be supposed to conduct himself with military precision. He breakfasted or dined when he pleased or when he could ; he slept when and where sleep overtook him. If his table was not always spread, his bed was always ready at the foot of some tree in the open forest. And in other respects Torres was not difficult to please. He had travelled during most of the morning, and having already eaten a little, he began to feel the want of a snooze. Two or three hours' rest would he thought, put him in a state to continue his road, and so he laid himself down on the grass as comfortably as he could, and waited for sleep beneath the ironwood-tree.

Torres was not one of those people who drop off to sleep without certain preliminaries. He was in the habit of drinking a drop or two of strong liquor, and of then smoking a pipe ; the spirits, he said, overexcited the brain‘ and the tobacco smoke agreeably mingled with the general haziness of his reverie.

Torres commenced, then, by applying to his lips a flask which he carried at his side ; it contained the liquor generally known under the name of "chica" in Peru, and more particularly under that of "caysuma" in the Upper Amazon, to which fermented distillation of the root of the sweet manioc the captain had added a good dose of "tafia," or native rum.

When Torres had drunk a little of this mixture he shook the flask, and discovered, not without regret, that it was nearly empty.

"Must get some more," he said very quietly.

Then taking out a short wooden pipe, he filled it with the coarse and bitter tobacco of Brazil, of which the leaves belong to that old "petun" introduced into France by Nicot, to whom we owe the popularization of the most productive and wide-spread of the solanaceæ.

This native tobacco had little in common with the fine qualities of our present manufacturers ; but Torres was not

Torres.

Page 11.

more difficult to please in this matter than in others, and so, having filled his pipe, he struck a match and applied the flame to a piece of that sticky substance which is the secretion of certain of the hymenoptera, and is known as "ants' amadou." With the amadou he lighted up, and after about a dozen whiffs his eyes closed, his pipe escaped from his fingers, and he fell asleep.

CHAPTER II.

ROBBER AND ROBBED.

TORRES slept for about half an hour, and then there was a noise amongst the trees—a sound of light footsteps, as though some visitor was walking with naked feet, and taking all the precaution he could lest he should be heard. To have put himself on guard against any suspicious approach would have been the first care of our adventurer had his eyes been open at the time. But he had not then awoke, and what advanced was able to arrive in his presence, at ten paces from the tree, without being perceived.

It was not a man at all, it was a " guariba."

Of all the prehensile-tailed mokeys which haunt the forests of the Upper Amazon—graceful sahuis, horned sapajous, grey-coated monos, sagouins which seem to wear a mask on their grimacing faces—the guariba is without doubt the most eccentric. Of sociable disposition, and not very savage, differing therein very greatly from the mucura, who is as ferocious as he is foul, he delights in company, and generally travels in troops. It was he whose presence had been signalled from afar by the monotonous concert of voices, so like the psalm-singing of some church choir. But if nature has not made him vicious, it is none the less necessary to attack him with caution, and under any circumstances a sleeping traveller ought not to leave himself exposed, lest a guariba should surprise him when he is not in a position to defend himself.

This monkey, which is also known in Brazil as the "barbado," was of large size. The suppleness and stoutness of his limbs proclaimed him a powerful creature, as fit to fight on the ground as to leap from branch to branch at the tops of the giants of the forest.

He advanced then cautiously, and with short steps. He glanced to the right and to the left, and rapidly swung his tail. To these representatives of the monkey tribe Nature has not been content to give four hands, she has shown herself more generous, and added a fifth, for the extremity of their caudal appendage possesses a perfect power of prehension.

The guariba noiselessly approached, brandishing a sturdy cudgel, which, wielded by his muscular arm, would have proved a formidable weapon. For some minutes he had seen the man at the foot of the tree, but the sleeper did not move, and this doubtless induced him to come and look at him a little nearer. He came forward then not without hesitation, and stopped at last about three paces off.

On his bearded face was pictured a grin, which showed his sharp-edged teeth, white as ivory, and the cudgel began to move about in a way that was not very reassuring for the captain of the woods.

Unmistakably the sight of Torres did not inspire the guariba with friendly thoughts. Had he then particular reasons for wishing evil to this defenceless specimen of the human race which chance had delivered over to him? Perhaps! We know how certain animals retain the memory of the bad treatment they have received, and it is possible that against backwoodsmen in general he bore some special grudge.

In fact Indians especially make more fuss about the monkey than any other kind of game, and, no matter to what species it belongs, follow its chase with the ardour of Nimrods, not only for the pleasure of hunting it, but for the pleasure of eating it.

Whatever it was, the guariba did not seem disinclined to change characters this time, and if he did not quite forget that nature had made him but a simple herbivore, and longed to devour the captain of the woods, he seemed at least to have made up his mind to get rid of one of his natural enemies.

After looking at him for some minutes the guariba

began to move round the tree. He stepped slowly, holding his breath, and getting nearer and nearer. His attitude
was threatening, his countenance ferocious. Nothing could
have seemed easier to him than to have crushed this
motionless man at a single blow, and assuredly at that
moment the life of Torres hung by a thread.

In truth the guariba stopped a second time close up to
the tree, placed himself at the side, so as to command the
head of the sleeper, and lifted his stick to give the blow.

But if Torres had been imprudent in putting near him
in the crevice of the root the little case which contained
his document and his fortune, it was this imprudence
which saved his life.

A sunbeam shooting between the branches just glinted
on the case, the polished metal of which lighted up like a
looking-glass. The monkey, with the frivolity peculiar to
his species, instantly had his attention distracted. His
ideas, if such an animal could have ideas, took another
direction. He stopped, caught hold of the case, jumped
back a pace or two, and, raising it to the level of his eyes,
looked at it not without surprise as he moved it about and
used it like a mirror. He was if anything still more
astonished when he heard the rattle of the gold pieces it
contained. The music enchanted him. It was like a rattle
in the hands of a child. He carried it to his mouth, and his
teeth grated against the metal, but made no impression on it.

Doubtless the guariba thought he had found some fruit of a new kind, a sort of huge almond brilliant all over, and with a kernel playing freely in its shell. But if he soon discovered his mistake he did not consider it a reason for throwing the case away; on the contrary, he grasped it more tightly in his left hand, and dropped the cudgel, which broke off a dry twig in its fall.

At this noise Torres woke, and with the quickness of those who are always on the watch, with whom there is no transition from the sleeping to the waking state, was immediately on his legs.

In an instant Torres had recognized with whom he had to deal.

"A guariba!" he cried.

And his hand seizing his manchetta, he put himself into a posture of defence.

The monkey, alarmed, jumped back at once, and not so brave before a waking man as a sleeping one, performed a rapid caper, and glided under the trees.

"It was time!" said Torres, "the rogue would have settled me without any ceremony!"

Of a sudden, between the hands of the monkey, who had stopped at about twenty paces, and was watching him with violent grimaces, as if he would like to snap his fingers at him, he caught sight of his precious case.

"The beggar!" he said. "If he has not killed me, he has done what is almost as bad. He has robbed me!"

The thought that the case held his money was not however, what then concerned him. But that which made him jump was the recollection that it contained the precious document, the loss of which was irreparable, as it carried with it that of all his hopes.

"Botheration!" cried he.

And at the moment, cost what it might to recapture his case, Torres threw himself in pursuit of the guariba.

He knew that to reach such an active animal was not easy. On the ground he could get away too fast, in the branches he could get away too far. A well-aimed gunshot could alone stop him as he ran or climbed, but Torres possessed no fire-arm. His sword-knife and hoe were useless unless he could get near enough to hit him.

It soon became evident that the monkey could not be reached unless by surprise. Hence Torres found it necessary to employ cunning in dealing with the mischievous animal. To stop, to hide himself behind some tree trunk, to disappear under a bush, might induce the guariba to pull up and retrace his steps, and there was nothing else for Torres to try. This was what he did, and the pursuit commenced under these conditions; but when the captain of the woods disappeared, the monkey patiently waited

C

until he came into sight again, and at this game Torres
fatigued himself without result.

"Confound the guariba!" he shouted at length. "There
will be no end to this, and he will lead me back to the
Brazilian frontier. If only he would let go of my case!
But no! The jingling of the money amuses him. Oh you
thief! If I could only get hold of you!"

And Torres recommenced the pursuit, and the monkey
scuttled off with renewed vigour.

An hour passed in this way without any result. Torres
showed a persistency which was quite natural. How without this document could he get his money?

And then anger seized him. He swore, he stamped, he
threatened the guariba. That annoying animal only
responded by a chuckling which was enough to put him
beside himself.

And then Torres gave himself up to the chase. He ran
at top speed, entangling himself in the high undergrowth,
among those thick brambles and interlacing creepers, across
which the guariba passed like a steeplechaser. Big roots
hidden beneath the grass lay often in the way. He
stumbled over them and again started in pursuit. At
length, to his astonishment, he found himself shouting,

"Come here! come here! you robber!" as if he could
make him understand him.

His strength gave out, breath failed him, and he was

The robber. Page 18.

obliged to stop. "Confound it!" said he, "when I am after runaway slaves across the jungle they never give me such trouble as this! But I will have you, you wretched monkey! I will go, yes, I will go as far as my legs will carry me, and we shall see!"

The guariba had remained motionless when he saw that the adventurer had ceased to pursue him. He rested also, for he had nearly reached that degree of exhaustion which had forbidden all movement on the part of Torres.

He remained like this during ten minutes, nibbling away at two or three roots, which he picked off the ground, and from time to time he rattled the case at his ear.

Torres, driven to distraction, picked up the stones within his reach and threw them at him, but did no harm at such a distance.

But he hesitated to make a fresh start. On the one hand, to keep on in chase of the monkey with so little chance of reaching him was madness. On the other, to accept as definite this accidental interruption to all his plans, to be not only conquered, but cheated and hoaxed by a dumb animal, was maddening. And in the meantime Torres had begun to think that when the night came the robber would disappear without trouble, and he, the robbed one, would find a difficulty in retracing his way through the dense forest. In fact, the pursuit had taken

C 2

him many miles from the bank of the river, and he would even now find it difficult to return to it.

Torres hesitated; he tried to resume his thoughts with coolness, and finally, after giving vent to a last imprecation, he was about to abandon all idea of regaining possession of his case, when once more, in spite of himself, there flashed across him the thought of his document, the remembrance of all that scaffolding on which his future hopes depended, on which he had counted so much; and he resolved to make another effort.

Then he got up.

The guariba got up too.

He made several steps in advance.

The monkey made as many in the rear, but this time, instead of plunging more deeply into the forest, he stopped at the foot of an enormous ficus—the tree of which the different kinds are so numerous all over the Upper Amazonian basin.

To seize the trunk with his four hands, to climb with the agility of a clown who is acting the monkey, to hook on with his prehensile tail to the first branches, which stretched away horizontally at forty feet from the ground, and to hoist himself to the top of the tree, to the point where the higher branches just bent beneath his weight, was only sport to the active guariba, and the work of but a few seconds.

Up there, installed at his ease, he resumed his interrupted repast, and gathered the fruits which were within his reach. Torres, like him, was much in want of something to eat and drink, but it was impossible! His pouch was flat, his flask was empty.

However, instead of retracing his steps he directed them towards the tree, although the position taken up by the monkey was still more unfavourable for him. He could not dream for one instant of climbing the ficus, which tho thief would have quickly abandoned for another.

And all the time the miserable case rattled at his ear.

Then in his fury, in his folly, Torres apostrophized the guariba. It would be impossible for us to tell the series of invectives in which he indulged. Not only did he call him a half-breed, which is the greatest of insults in the mouth of a Brazilian of white descent, but " curiboca "—that is to say, half-breed negro and Indian, and of all the insults that one man can hurl at another in this equatorial latitude "curiboca" is the cruellest.

But the monkey, who was only a humble quadruman, was simply amused at what would have revolted a representative of humanity.

Then Torres began to throw stones at him again, and bits of roots and everything he could get hold of that would do for a missile. Had he the hope to seriously hurt the monkey? No! he no longer knew what he was about.

To tell the truth, anger at his powerlessness had deprived him of his wits. Perhaps he hoped that in one of the movements which the guariba would make in passing from branch to branch the case might escape him, perhaps he thought that if he continued to worry the monkey he might throw it at his head. But no! the monkey did not part with the case, and, holding it with one hand, he had still three left with which to move.

Torres, in despair, was just about to abandon the chase for good, and to return towards the Amazon, when he heard the sound of voices. Yes! the sound of human voices.

These were speaking at about twenty paces to the right of him.

The first care of Torres was to hide himself in a dense thicket. Like a prudent man, he did not wish to show himself without at least knowing with whom he might have to deal. Panting, puzzled, his ears on the stretch, he waited, when suddenly the sharp report of a gun rang through the woods.

A cry followed, and the monkey, mortally wounded, fell heavily on the ground, still holding Torres' case.

"By Jove!" he muttered, "that bullet came at the right time!"

And then, without fearing to be seen, he came out of the thicket, and two young gentlemen appeared from under the trees.

The young Brazilians.

Page 23.

They were Brazilians clothed as hunters, with leather boots, light palm-leaf hats, waistcoats, or rather tunics, buckled in at the waist, and more convenient than the national poncho. By their features and their complexion they were at once recognizable as of Portuguese descent.

Each of them was armed with one of those long guns of Spanish make which slightly remind us of the arms of the Arabs, guns of long range and considerable precision, which the dwellers in the forest of the Upper Amazon handle with success.

What had just happened was a proof of this. At an angular distance of more than eighty paces the quadruman had been shot full in the head.

The two young men carried in addition, in their belts, a sort of dagger-knife, which is known in Brazil as a " foca," and which hunters do not hesitate to use when attacking the ounce and other wild animals, which, if not very formidable, are pretty numerous in these forests.

Torres had obviously little to fear from this meeting, and so he went on running towards the monkey's corpse.

But the young men, who were taking the same direction, had less ground to cover, and coming forward a few paces, found themselves face to face with Torres.

The latter had recovered his presence of mind.

"Many thanks, gentlemen," said he, gaily, as he raised the brim of his hat; "in killing this wretched animal you have just done me a great service!"

The hunters looked at him inquiringly, not knowing what value to attach to his thanks.

Torres explained matters in a few words.

"You thought you had killed a monkey," said he, "but as it happens you have killed a thief!"

"If we have been of use to you," said the youngest of the two, "it was by accident, but we are none the less pleased to find that we have done some good."

And, taking several steps to the rear, he bent over the guariba, and, not without an effort, withdrew the case from his stiffened hand.

"Doubtless that, sir, is what belongs to you?"

"The very thing," said Torres, briskly, catching hold of the case and failing to repress a huge sigh of relief.

"Whom ought I to thank, gentlemen," said he, "for the service you have rendered me?"

"My friend, Manoel, assistant-surgeon, Brazilian army," replied the young man.

"If it was I who shot the monkey, Benito," said Manoel, "it was you that pointed him out to me."

"In that case, sirs," replied Torres, "I am under an obligation to you both, as well to you, Mr. Manoel, as to you, Mr.——?"

"Benito Garral," replied Manoel.

The captain of the woods required great command over himself to avoid giving a jump when he heard this name, and more especially when the young man obligingly continued,—

"My father, Joam Garral, has his farm about three miles from here. If you would like, Mr.——?"

"Torres," replied the adventurer.

"If you would like to accompany us there, Mr. Torres, you will be hospitably received."

"I do not know that I can," said Torres, who, surprised by this unexpected meeting, hesitated to make a start. "I fear in truth that I am not able to accept your offer. The occurrence I have just related to you has caused me to lose time. It is necessary for me to return at once to the Amazon—as I purpose descending thence to Para."

"Very well, Mr. Torres," replied Benito, "it is not unlikely that we shall see you again in our travels, for before a month has passed my father and all his family will have taken the same road as you."

"Ah!" said Torres, sharply, "your father is thinking of recrossing the Brazilian frontier?"

"Yes, for a voyage of some months," replied Benito. "At least we hope to make 'him decide so. Don't we, Manoel?"

Manoel nodded affirmatively.

"Well, gentlemen," replied Torres, "it is very probable that we shall meet again on the road. But I cannot, much to my regret, accept your offer now. I thank you, nevertheless, and I consider myself as twice your debtor."

And having said so, Torres saluted the young men, who in turn saluted him, and set out on their way to the farm.

As for Torres, he looked after them as they got farther and farther away, and when he had lost sight of them,—

"Ah! he is about to recross the frontier!" said he, with a deep voice. "Let him recross it! and he will be still more at my mercy! Pleasant journey to you, Joam Garral!"

And having uttered these words, the captain of the woods, making for the south so as to regain the left bank of the river by the shortest road, disappeared into the dense forest.

CHAPTER III.

THE GARRAL FAMILY.

THE village of Iquitos is situated on the left bank of the Amazon, near the seventy-fourth meridian, on that portion of the great river which still bears the name of the Marâ-non, and of which the bed separates Peru from the Republic of Ecuador. It is about five-and-fifty leagues to the west of the Brazilian frontier.

Iquitos, like every other collection of huts, hamlet, or village, met with in the basin of the Upper Amazon, was founded by the missionaries. Up to the seventeenth year of the century the Iquito Indians, who then formed the entire population, were settled in the interior of the province at some distance from the river. But one day the springs in their territory all dried up under the influence of a volcanic eruption, and they were obliged to come and take up their abode on the left of the Marânon. The race soon altered through the alliances which were entered into with the riverine Indians, Ticunas, or Omaguas, mixed

descent with a few Spaniards, and to-day Iquitos has a
population of two or three families of half-breeds.

The village is most picturesquely grouped on a kind of
esplanade, and runs along at about sixty feet from the
river. It consists of some forty miserable huts, whose
thatched roofs only just render them worthy of the name
of cottages. A stairway made of crossed trunks of trees
leads up to the village, which lies hidden from the traveller's
eyes until the steps have been ascended. Once at the top
he finds himself before an enclosure admitting of slight
defence, and consisting of many different shrubs and arborescent plants, attached to each other by festoons of
lianas, which here and there have made their way above
the summits of the graceful palms and banana-trees.

At the time we speak of the Indians of Iquitos went
about in almost a state of nudity. The Spaniards and
half-breeds alone were clothed, and much as they scorned
their indigenous fellow-citizens, wore only a simple shirt,
light cotton trousers, and a straw hat. All lived cheerlessly
enough in the village, mixing little together, and if they
did meet occasionally, it was only at such times as the
bell of the mission called them to the dilapidated cottage
which served them for a church.

But if existence in the village of Iquitos, as in most of
the hamlets of the Upper Amazon, was almost in a rudi-
mentary stage, it was only necessary to journey a league

Iquitos.

Page 28.

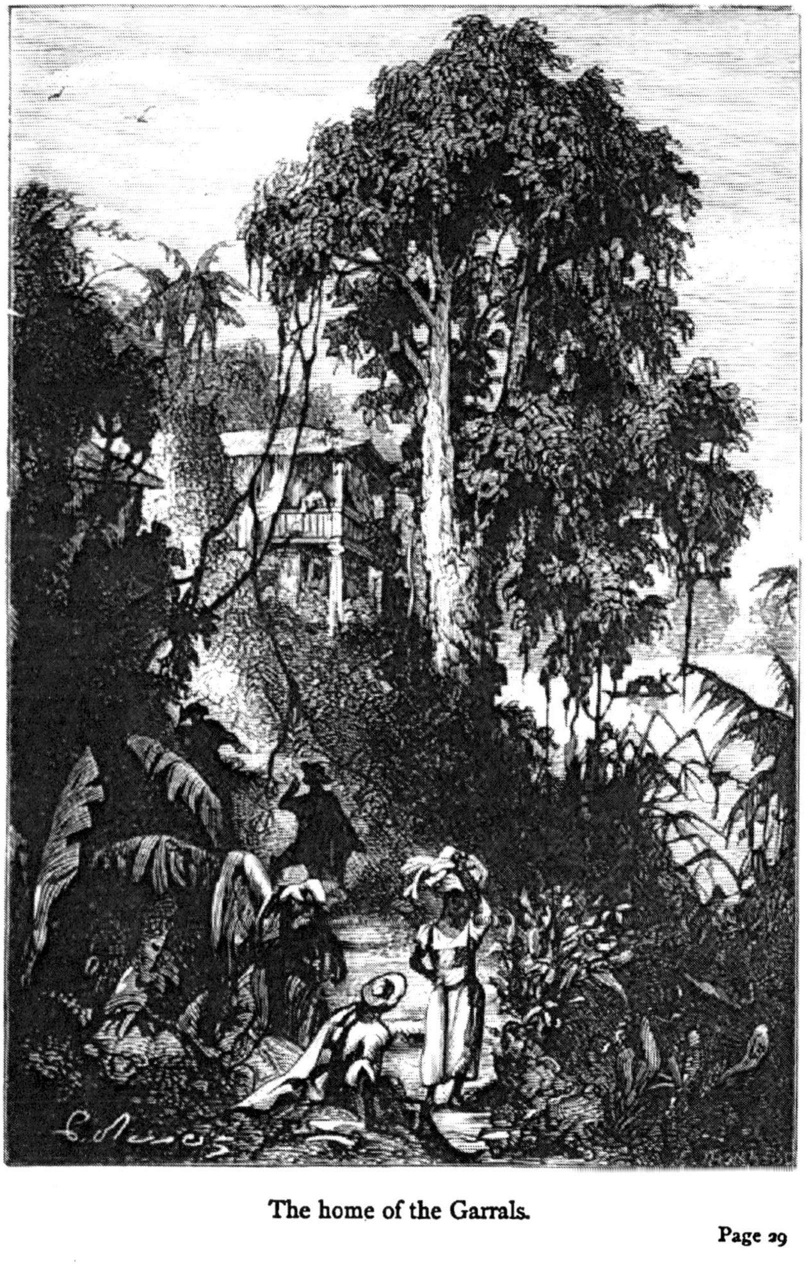

The home of the Garrals.

Page 29

farther down the river to find on the same bank a wealthy settlement, with all the elements of comfortable life.

This was the farm of Joam Garral, towards which our two young friends returned after their meeting with the captain of the woods.

There, on a bend of the stream, at the junction of the River Nanay, which is here about 500 feet across, there had been established for many years this farm, homestead, or, to use the expression of the country, "fazenda," then in the height of its prosperity. The Nanay with its left bank bounded it to the north for about a mile, and for nearly the same distance to the east it ran along the bank of the larger river. To the west some small rivulets, tributaries of the Nanay, and some lagoons of small extent, separated it from the savannah and the fields devoted to the pasturage of the cattle.

It was here that Joam Garral, in 1826, twenty-six years before the date when our story opens, was received by the proprietor of the fazenda.

This Portuguese, whose name was Magalhaës, followed the trade of timber-felling, and his settlement, then recently formed, extended for about half a mile along the bank of the river.

There, hospitable as he was like all the Portuguese of the old race, Magalhaës lived with his daughter Yaquita, who after the death of her mother had taken charge of his household. Magalhaës was an excellent worker, inured to fatigue, but lacking education. If he understood the management of the few slaves whom he owned, and the dozen Indians whom he hired, he showed himself much less apt in the various external requirements of his trade. In truth, the establishment at Iquitos was not prospering, and the affairs of the Portuguese were getting somewhat embarrassed.

It was under these circumstances that Joam Garral, then twenty-two years old, found himself one day in the presence of Magalhaës. He had arrived in the country at the limit both of his strength and his resources. Magalhaës had found him half dead with hunger and fatigue in the neighbouring forest. The Portuguese had an excellent heart : he did not ask the unknown where he came from, but what he wanted. The noble, high-spirited look which Joam Garral bore in spite of his exhaustion, had touched him. He received him, restored him, and, for several days to begin with, offered him a hospitality which lasted for his life.

Under such conditions it was that Joam Garral was introduced to the farm at Iquitos.

Brazilian by birth, Joam Garral was without family or fortune. Trouble, he said, had obliged him to quit his country and abandon all thoughts of return. He asked his host to excuse his entering on his past misfortunes—misfortunes as serious as they were unmerited. What he sought, and what he wished was a new life, a life of labour. He had started on his travels with some slight thought of entering a fazenda in the interior. He was educated, intelligent. He had in all his bearing that inexpressible something which tells you that the man is genuine and of frank and upright character. Magalhaës, quite taken with him, asked him to remain at the farm, where he would, in a measure, supply that which was wanting in the worthy farmer.

Joam Garral accepted the offer without hesitation. His intention had been to join a "seringal," or caoutchouc concern, in which in those days a good workman could earn from five to six piastres a day, and could hope to become a master if he had any luck; but Magalhaës very truly observed that if the pay was good, work was only found in the seringals at harvest time—that is to say, during only a few months of the year—and this would not constitute the permanent position that a young man ought to wish for.

The Portuguese was right. Joam Garral saw it, and entered resolutely into the service of the fazenda, deciding to devote to it all his powers.

Magalhaës had no cause to regret his generous action. His business recovered. His wood trade, which extended by means of the Amazon up to Para, was soon considerably extended under the impulse of Joam Garral. The fazenda began to grow in proportion, and to spread out along the bank of the river up to its junction with the Nanay. A delightful residence was made of the house; it was raised a storey, surrounded by a verandah, and half hidden under beautiful trees—mimosas, fig-sycamores, bauhinias, and paullinias, whose trunks were invisible beneath a network of scarlet-flowered bromelias and passion-flowers.

At a distance, behind huge bushes and a dense mass of arborescent plants, were concealed the buildings in which the staff of the fazenda were accommodated—the servants' offices, the cabins of the blacks, and the huts of the Indians. From the bank of the river, bordered with reeds and aquatic plants, the tree-encircled house was alone visible.

A vast meadow, laboriously cleared along the lagoons, offered excellent pasturage. Cattle abounded—a new source of profit in these fertile countries, where a herd doubles in four years, and where ten per cent. interest is earned by nothing more than the skins and the hides of the animals killed for the consumption of those who raise them! A few "sitios," or manioc and coffee plantations, were started in parts of the woods which were cleared. Fields of sugar-canes soon required the construction of a mill to crush the sacchariferous stalks destined to be used hereafter in the manufacture of molasses, tafia, and rum. In short, ten years after the arrival of Joam Garral at the farm at Iquitos the fazenda had become one of the richest establishments on the Upper Amazon. Thanks to the good management exercised by the young clerk over the works at home and the business abroad, its prosperity daily increased.

The Portuguese did not wait so long to acknowledge what he owed to Joam Garral. In order to recompense him in proportion to his merits he had from the first given him an interest in the profits of his business, and four years after his arrival he had made him a partner on the same footing as himself, and with equal shares.

But there was more that he had in store for him. Yaquita, his daughter, had, in this silent young man, so gentle to others, so stern to himself, recognized the sterling qualities which her father had done. She was in love with him, but though on his side Joam had not remained insensible to the merits and the beauty of this excellent girl, he was too proud and reserved to dream of asking her to marry him.

A serious incident hastened the solution.

Magalhaës was one day superintending a clearance and was mortally wounded by the fall of a tree. Carried home helpless to the farm, and feeling himself lost, he raised up Yaquita, who was weeping by his side, took her hand, and put it into that of Joam Garral, making him swear to take her for his wife.

D

"You have re-made my fortune," he said, "and I shall not die in peace unless by this union I know that the fortune of my daughter is assured."

"I can continue her devoted servant, her brother, her protector, without being her husband," Joam Garral had at first replied. "I owe you all, Magalhaës. I will never forget it, but the price you would pay for my endeavours is out of all proportion to what they are worth."

The old man insisted. Death would not allow him to wait; he demanded the promise, and it was made to him.

Yaquita was then twenty-two years old, Joam was twenty-six. They loved each other, and they were married some hours before the death of Magalhaës, who had just strength left to bless their union.

It was under these circumstances that in 1830 Joam Garral became the new fazender of Iquitos, to the immense satisfaction of all those who composed the staff of the farm.

The prosperity of the settlement could not do otherwise than grow when these two minds were thus united.

A year after her marriage Yaquita presented her husband with a son, and, two years after, a daughter. Benito and Minha, the grandchildren of the old Portuguese, became worthy of their grandfather, children worthy of Joam and Yaquita.

The daughter grew to be one of the most charming of

The death of Magalhäes.

Page 34.

girls. She never left the fazenda. Brought up in pure and healthy surroundings, in the midst of the beauteous nature of the tropics, the education given to her by her mother, and the instruction received by her from her father, were ample. What more could she have learnt in a convent at Manaos or Belem? Where would she have found better examples of the domestic virtues? Would her mind and feelings have been more delicately formed away from her home? If it was ordained that she was not to succeed her mother in the management of the fazenda, she was equal to any other position to which she might be called.

With Benito it was another thing. His father very wisely wished him to receive as solid and complete an education as could then be obtained in the large towns of Brazil. There was nothing which the rich fazender refused his son. Benito was possessed of a cheerful disposition, an active mind, a lively intelligence, and qualities of heart equal to those of his head. At the age of twelve he was sent into Para, to Belem, and there, under the direction of excellent professors, he acquired the elements of an education which could not but eventually make him a distinguished man. Nothing in literature, in the sciences, in the arts, was a stranger to him. He studied as if the fortune of his father would not allow him to remain idle. He was not among such as imagine that riches exempt men from work—he was one of those noble characters, re-

solute and just, who believe that nothing should diminish
our natural obligation in this respect if we wish to be
worthy of the name of men.

During the first years of his residence at Belem, Benito
had made the acquaintance of Manoel Valdez. This young
man, the son of a merchant in Para, was pursuing his
studies in the same institution as Benito. The conformity
of their characters and their tastes proved no barrier to
their uniting in the closest of friendships, and they became
inseparable companions.

Manoel, born in 1832, was one year older than Benito.
He had only a mother, and she lived on the modest fortune which her husband had left her. When Manoel's
preliminary studies were finished, he had taken up the
subject of medicine. He had a passionate taste for that
noble profession, and his intention was to enter the army,
towards which he felt himself attracted.

At the time that we saw him with his friend Benito,
Manoel Valdez had already obtained his first step, and he
had come away on leave for some months to the fazenda,
where he was accustomed to pass his holidays. Well-built,
and of distinguished bearing, with a certain native pride
which became him well, the young man was treated by
Joam and Yaquita as another son. But if this quality of
son made him the brother of Benito, the title was scarcely
appreciated by him when Minha was concerned, for he

soon became attached to the young girl by a bond more intimate than could exist between brother and sister.

In the year 1852—of which four months had already passed before the commencement of this history—Joam Garral attained the age of forty-eight years. In that sultry climate, which wears men away so quickly, he had known how, by sobriety, self-denial, suitable living, and constant work, to remain untouched where others had prematurely succumbed. His hair, which he wore short, and his beard, which was full, had already grown grey, and gave him the look of a puritan. The proverbial honesty of the Brazilian merchants and fazenders showed itself in his features, of which straightforwardness was the leading characteristic. His calm temperament seemed to indicate an interior fire, kept well under control. The fearlessness of his look denoted a deep-rooted strength, to which, when danger threatened, he could never appeal in vain.

But, notwithstanding, one could not help remarking about this quiet man of vigorous health, with whom all things had succeeded in life, a depth of sadness which even the tenderness of Yaquita had not been able to subdue.

Respected by all, placed in all the conditions that would seem necessary to happiness, why was not this just man more cheerful and less reserved ? Why did he seem to be happy for others and not for himself ? Was this disposition attributable to some secret grief? Herein was a constant source of anxiety to his wife.

Yaquita was now forty-four. In that tropical country where women are already old at thirty she had learnt the secret of resisting the climate's destructive influences, and her features a little sharpened, but still beautiful, retained the haughty outline of the Portuguese type, in which nobility of face unites so naturally with dignity of mind.

Benito and Minha responded with an affection unbounded and unceasing for the love which their parents bore them.

Benito was now aged one-and-twenty, and quick, brave, and sympathetic, contrasted outwardly with his friend Manoel, who was more serious and reflective. It was a great treat for Benito, after quite a year passed at Belem, so far from the fazenda, to return with his young friend to his home to see once more his father, his mother, his sister, and to find himself, enthusiastic hunter as he was, in the midst of these superb forests of the Upper Amazon, some of whose secrets remained after so many centuries still unsolved by man.

Minha was twenty years old. A lovely girl, brunette, and with large blue eyes, eyes which seemed to open into her very soul; of middle height, good figure, and winning grace, in every way the very image of Yaquita. A little more serious than her brother, affable, good-natured, and

Minha and Lina.

Page 38.

charitable, she was beloved by all. On this subject you could fearlessly interrogate the humblest servants of the fazenda. It was unnecessary to ask her brother's friend, Manoel Valdez, what he thought of her! He was too much interested in the question to have replied without a certain amount of partiality.

This sketch of the Garral family would not be complete, and would lack some of its features, were we not to mention the numerous staff of the fazenda.

In the first place, then, it behoves us to name an old negress, of some sixty years, called Cybele, free through the will of her master, a slave through her affection for him and his, and who had been the nurse of Yaquita. She was one of the family. She thee-ed and thou-ed both daughter and mother. The whole of this good creature's life was passed in these fields, in the middle of these forests, on that bank of the river which bounded the horizon of the farm. Coming as a child to Iquitos in the slave-trading times, she had never quitted the village; she was married there, and early a widow, had lost her only son, and remained in the service of Magalhaës. Of the Amazon she knew no more than what flowed before her eyes.

With her, and more specially attached to the service of Minha, was a pretty, laughing mulatto, of the same age as her mistress, to whom she was completely devoted. She was called Lina. One of those gentle creatures, a little spoiled perhaps, to whom a good deal of familiarity is allowed but who in return adore their mistresses. Quick, restless, coaxing, and lazy, she could do what she pleased in the house.

As for servants they were of two kinds—Indians, of whom there were about a hundred, employed always for the works of the fazenda, and blacks to about double the number, who were not yet free, but whose children were not born slaves. Joam Garral had herein preceded the Brazilian Government. In this country, moreover, the negroes coming from Benguela, the Congo, or the Gold Coast were always treated with kindness, and it was not at the fazenda of Iquitos that one would look for those sad examples of cruelty which were so frequent on foreign plantations.

CHAPTER IV.

HESITATION.

MANOEL was in love with the sister of his friend Benito, and she was in love with him. Each was sensible of the other's worth, and each was worthy of the other.

When he was no longer able to mistake the state of his feelings towards Minha, Manoel had opened his heart to Benito.

"Manoel, my friend," had immediately answered the enthusiastic young fellow, "you could not do better than wish to marry my sister. Leave it to me! I will commence by speaking to the mother, and I think I can promise that you will not have to wait long for her consent!"

Half an hour afterwards he had done so.

Benito had nothing to tell his mother which she did not know; Yaquita had already divined the young people's secret.

Before ten minutes had elapsed Benito was in the presence of Minha. They had but to agree; there was no need for much eloquence. At the first words the head of the gentle girl was laid on her brother's shoulder, and the confession, "I am so happy!" was whispered from her heart.

The answer almost came before the question; that was obvious. Benito did not ask for more.

There could be little doubt as to Joam Garral's consent. But if Yaquita and her children did not at once speak to him about the marriage, it was because they wished at the same time to touch on a question which might be more difficult to solve. That question was, Where should the wedding take place?

Where should it be celebrated? In the humble cottage which served for the village church? Why not? Joam and Yaquita had there received the nuptial benediction of the Padre Passanha, who was then the curate of Iquitos parish. At that time, as now, there was no distinction in Brazil between the civil and religious acts, and the registers of the mission were sufficient testimony to a ceremony which no officer of the civil power was entrusted to attend to.

Joam Garral would probably wish the marriage to take place at Iquitos, with grand ceremonies, and the attendance of the whole staff of the fazenda, but if such was to be his idea he would have to withstand a vigorous attack concerning it.

"Manoel," Minha had said to her betrothed, "if I was consulted in the matter we should not be married here, but at Para. Madame Valdez is an invalid ; she cannot visit Iquitos, and I should not like to become her daughter without knowing and being known by her. My mother agrees with me in thinking so. We should like to persuade my father to take us to Belem. Do you not think so ? "

To this proposition Manoel had replied by pressing Minha's hand. He also had a great wish for his mother to be present at his marriage. Benito had approved the scheme without hesitation, and it was only necessary to persuade Joam Garral. And hence on this day the young men had gone out hunting in the woods, so as to leave Yaquita alone with her husband.

In the afternoon these two were in the large room of the house. Joam Garral, who had just come in, was half reclining on a couch of plaited bamboos, when Yaquita, a little anxious, came and seated herself beside him.

To tell Joam of the feelings which Manoel entertained towards his daughter was not what troubled her. The happiness of Minha could not but be assured by the marriage, and Joam would be glad to welcome to his arms the new son whose sterling qualities he recognized and appreciated. But to persuade her husband to leave the fazenda Yaquita felt to be a very serious matter.

In fact, since Joam Garral, then a young man, had arrived in the country, he had never left it for a day.

Though the sight of the Amazon, with its waters gently flowing to the east, invited him to follow its course; though Joam every year sent rafts of wood to Manaos, to Belem, and the seacoast of Para; though he had seen each year Benito leave after his holidays to return to his studies, yet the thought seemed never to have occurred to him to go with him.

The products of the farm, of the forest, and of the fields, the fazender sold on the spot. He had no wish, either with thought or look, to go beyond the horizon which bounded his Eden.

From this it followed that for five-and-twenty years Joam Garral had never crossed the Brazilian frontier, his wife and daughter had never set foot on Brazilian soil. The longing to see something of that beautiful country of which Benito was often talking was not wanting, nevertheless. Two or three times Yaquita had sounded her husband in the matter. But she had noticed that the thought of leaving the fazenda, if only for a few weeks, brought an increase of sadness to his face. His eyes would close, and, in a tone of mild reproach, he would answer,—

"Why leave our home? Are we not comfortable here?"

And Yaquita, in the presence of the man whose active kindness and unchangeable tenderness rendered her so happy, had not the courage to persist.

This time, however, there was a serious reason to make it worth while. The marriage of Minha afforded an excellent opportunity, it being so natural for them to accompany her to Belem, where she was going to live with her husband. She would there see and learn to love the mother of Manoel Valdez. How could Joam Garral hesitate in the face of so praiseworthy a desire? Why, on the other hand, did he not participate in this desire to become acquainted with her who was to be the second mother of his child?

Yaquita took her husband's hand, and with that gentle voice which had been to him all the music of his life,—

"Joam," she said, "I am going to talk to you about something which we ardently wish, and which will make you as happy as we are."

"What is it about, Yaquita?" asked Joam.

"Manoel loves your daughter, he is loved by her, and in this union they will find the happiness—"

At the first words of Yaquita Joam Garral had risen, without being able to control a sudden start. His eyes were immediately cast down, and he seemed to designedly avoid the look of his wife.

"What is the matter with you?" asked she.

"Minha? To get married!" murmured Joam.

"My dear," said Yaquita, feeling somewhat hurt, "have you any objection to make to the marriage? Have you not for some time noticed the feelings which Manoel has entertained towards our daughter ? "

" Yes ; and a year since—"

And Joam sat down without finishing his thoughts. By an effort of his will he had again become master of himself. The unaccountable impression which had been made upon him disappeared. Gradually his eyes returned to meet those of Yaquita, and he remained thoughtfully looking at her.

Yaquita took his hand.

" Joam," she said, " have I been deceived ? Had you no idea that this marriage would one day take place, and that it would give her every chance of happiness ? "

" Yes," answered Joam. " All ! Certainly ! But, Yaquita, this wedding—this wedding that we are both thinking of—when is it coming off? Shortly ? "

" It will come off when you choose, Joam."

" And it will take place here—at Iquitos ? "

This question obliged Yaquita to enter on the other matter which she had at heart. She did not do so, however, without some hesitation, which was quite intelligible.

" Joam," said she, after a moment's silence, " listen to me. Regarding this wedding, I have got a proposal which I hope you will approve of. Two or three times during the last twenty years I have asked you to take me and my daughter to the provinces of the Lower Amazon, and to

Para, where we have never been. The cares of the fazenda, the works which have required your presence, have not allowed you to grant our request. To absent yourself even for a few days would then have injured your business. But now everything has been successful beyond your dreams, and if the hour of repose has not yet come for you, you can at least for a few weeks get away from your work."

Joam Garral did not answer, but Yaquita felt his hand tremble in hers, as though under the shock of some sorrowful recollection. At the same time a half-smile came to her husband's lips—a mute invitation for her to finish what she had begun.

"Joam," she continued "here is an occasion which we shall never see again in this life. Minha is going to be married away from us, and is going to leave us! It is the first sorrow which our daughter has caused us, and my heart quails when I think of the separation which is so near! But I should be content if I could accompany her to Belem! Does it not seem right to you, even in other respects, that we should know her husband's mother, who is to replace me, and to whom we are about to entrust her? Added to this, Minha does not wish to grieve Madame Valdez by getting married at a distance from her. When we were married, Joam, if your mother had been alive, would you not have liked her to be present at your wedding?"

At these words of Yaquita Joam made a movement which he could not repress.

"My dear," continued Yaquita, "with Minha, with our two sons, Benito and Manoel, with you, how I should like to see Brazil, and to journey down this splendid river, even to the provinces on the sea-coast through which it runs! It seems to me that the separation would be so much less cruel! As we came back we should revisit our daughter in her house with her second mother. I would not think of her as gone I knew not where. I would fancy myself much less a stranger to the doings of her life."

This time Joam had fixed his eyes on his wife and looked at her for some time without saying anything.

What ailed him? Why this hesitation to grant a request which was so just in itself—to say "Yes," when it would give such pleasure to all who belonged to him? His business affairs could not afford a sufficient reason. A few weeks of absence would not compromise matters to such a degree. His manager would be able to take his place without any hitch in the fazenda. And yet all this time he hesitated.

Yaquita had taken both her husband's hands in hers, and pressed them tenderly.

"Joam," she said, "it is not a mere whim that I am asking you to grant. No! For a long time I have thought over the proposition I have just made to you; and if you

At the door.

Page 49.

consent, it will be the realization of my most cherished desire. Our children know why I am now talking to you. Minha, Benito, Manoel, all ask this favour, that we should accompany them. We would all rather have the wedding at Belem than at Iquitos. It will be better for our daughter, for her establishment, for the position which she will take at Belem, that she should arrive with her people, and appear less of a stranger in the town in which she will spend most of her life."

Joam Garral leant on his elbows. For a moment he hid his face in his hands, like a man who had to collect his thoughts before he made answer. There was evidently some hesitation which he was anxious to overcome, even some trouble which his wife felt but could not explain. A secret battle was being fought under that thoughtful brow. Yaquita got anxious, and almost reproached herself for raising the question. Anyhow, she was resigned to what Joam should decide. If the expedition would cost too much, she would silence her wishes; she would never more speak of leaving the fazenda, and never ask the reason for the inexplicable refusal.

Some minutes passed. Joam Garral rose. He went to the door, and did not return. Then he seemed to give a last look on that glorious nature, on that corner of the world where for twenty years of his life he had met with all his happiness.

E

Then with slow steps he returned to his wife. His face bore a new expression, that of a man who had taken a last decision, and with whom irresolution had ceased.

"You are right," he said, in a firm voice. "The journey is necessary. When shall we start?"

"Ah! Joam! my Joam!" cried Yaquita, in her joy. "Thank you for me! Thank you for them!"

And tears of affection came to her eyes as her husband clasped her to his heart.

At this moment happy voices were heard outside at the door of the house.

Manoel and Benito appeared an instant after at the threshold, almost at the same moment as Minha entered the room.

"Children! your father consents!" cried Yaquita. "We are going to Belem!"

With a grave face, and without speaking a word, Joam Garral received the congratulations of his son and the kisses of his daughter.

"And what date, father," asked Benito, "have you fixed for the wedding?"

"Date?" answered Joam. "Date? We shall see. We will fix it at Belem."

"I am so happy! I am so happy!" repeated Minha, as she had done on the day when she had first known of Manoel's request. "We shall now see the Amazon in all its glory throughout its course through the provinces of Brazil! Thanks, father!"

And the young enthusiast, whose imagination was already stirred, continued to her brother and to Manoel,—

"Let us be off to the library! Let us get hold of every book and every map that we can find which will tell us anything about this magnificent river-system! Don't let us travel like blind folks! I want to see everything and know everything about this king of the rivers of the earth!"

CHAPTER V.

THE AMAZON.

"THE largest river in the whole world!" said Benito to Manoel Valdez, on the morrow.

They were sitting on the bank which formed the southern boundary of the fazenda, and looking at the liquid molecules passing slowly by, which, coming from the enormous range of the Andes, were on their road to lose themselves in the Atlantic Ocean eight hundred leagues away.

"And the river which carries to the sea the largest volume of water!" replied Manoel.

"A volume so considerable," added Benito, "that it freshens the sea-water for an immense distance from its mouth, and the force of whose current is felt by ships at eight leagues from the coast!"

"A river whose course is developed over more than thirty degrees of latitude!"

"And in a basin which from south to north does not comprise less than twenty-five degrees!"

On the bank of the river.

Page 52.

"A basin!" exclaimed Benito. "Can you call it a basin, the vast plain through which it runs, the savannah which on all sides stretches out of sight, without a hill to give a gradient, without a mountain to bound the horizon?"

"And along its whole extent," continued Manoel, "like the thousand tentacles of some gigantic polyp, two hundred tributaries, flowing from north or south, themselves fed by smaller affluents without number, by the side of which the large rivers of Europe are but petty streamlets."

"And in its course 560 islands, without counting islets, drifting or stationary, forming a kind of archipelago, and yielding of themselves the wealth of a kingdom!"

"And along its flanks canals, lagoons, and lakes, such as cannot be met with even in Switzerland, Lombardy, Scotland, or Canada."

"A river which, fed by its myriad tributaries, discharges into the Atlantic over 250 millions of cubic metres of water every hour."

"A river whose course serves as the boundary of two republics, and sweeps majestically across the largest empire of South America, as if it were, in very truth, the Pacific Ocean itself flowing out along its own canal into the Atlantic."

"And what a mouth! An arm of the sea in which one

island, Marajo, has a circumference of more than 500 leagues!"

"And whose waters the ocean does not pond back without raising in a strife which is phenomenal, a tide-race, or 'pororoca,' to which the ebbs, the bores, and the eddies of other rivers are but tiny ripples fanned up by the breeze."

"A river which three names are scarcely enough to distinguish, and which ships of heavy tonnage, without any change in their cargoes, can ascend for more that 3000 miles from its mouth."

"A river which, by itself, its affluents, and subsidiary streams, opens a navigable commercial route across the whole of the south of the continent, passing from the Magdalena to the Ortequazza, from the Ortequazza to the Caqueta, from the Caqueta to the Putumayo, from the Putumayo to the Amazon! Four thousand miles of water-way, which only require a few canals to make the network of navigation complete!"

"In short, the biggest and most admirable river-system which we have in the world."

The two young men were speaking in a kind of frenzy of their incomparable river. They were themselves children of this great Amazon, whose affluents, well worthy of itself, from the highways which penetrate Bolivia, Peru, Ecuador, New Grenada, Venezuela, and the four Guianas —English, French, Dutch, and Brazilian.

What nations, what races, has it seen whose origin is lost in the far-distant past! It is one of the largest rivers of the globe. Its true source still baffles our explorers. Numbers of States still claim the honour of giving it birth. The Amazon was not likely to escape the inevitable fate, and Peru, Ecuador, and Columbia have for years disputed as to the honour of its glorious paternity.

To-day, however, there seems to be little doubt but that the Amazon rises in Peru, in the district of Huaraco, in the department of Tarma, and that it starts from the Lake of Lauricocha, which is situated between the eleventh and twelfth degree of south latitude.

Those who make the river rise in Bolivia, and descend from the mountains of Titicaca, have to prove that the true Amazon is the Ucayali, which is formed by the junction of the Paro and the Apurimac—an assertion which is now generally rejected.

At its departure from Lake Lauricocha the youthful river starts towards the north-east for a distance of 560 miles, and does not strike to the west until it has received an important tributary—the Panta. It is called the Marañon in its journey through Columbia and Peru up to the Brazilian frontier—or, rather, the Maranhão, for Marañon is only the French rendering of the Portuguese name.

From the frontier of Brazil to Manaos, where the superb Rio Negro joins it, it takes the name of the Solimaës, or

Solimoens, from the name of the Indian tribe Solimao, of which survivors are still found in the neighbouring provinces. And, finally, from Manaos to the sea it is the Amasenas, or river of the Amazons, a name given it by the old Spaniards, the descendants of the adventurous Orellana, whose vague but enthusiastic stories went to show that there existed a tribe of female warriors on the Rio Nhamunda, one of the middle-sized affluents of the great river.

From its commencement the Amazon is recognizable as destined to become a magnificent stream. There are neither rapids nor obstacles of any sort until it reaches a defile where its course is slightly narrowed between two picturesque and unequal precipices. No falls are met with until this point is reached, where it curves to the eastward, and passes through the intermediary chain of the Andes. Hereabouts are a few waterfalls, were it not for which the river would be navigable from its mouth to its source. As it is, however, according to Humboldt, the Amazon is free for five-sixths of its length.

And from its first starting there is no lack of tributaries, which are themselves fed by subsidiary streams. There is the Chinchipa, coming from the north-east, on its left. On its right it is joined by the Chachapoyas, coming from north-east. On the left we have the Marona and the Pastuca; and the Guallaga comes in from the right near the mission-station of Laguna. On the left there comes the Chambyra and the Tigré, flowing from north-east; and on the right the Huallaga, which joins the main stream 2800 miles from the Atlantic, and can be ascended by steamboats for over 200 miles into the very heart of Peru. To the right, again, near the mission of San Joachim d'Omaguas, just where the upper basin terminates, and after flowing majestically across the pampas of Sacramento, it receives the magnificent Ucayali, the great artery which, fed by numerous affluents, descends from Lake Chucuito, in the north-east of Arica.

Such are the principal branches above the village of Iquitos. Down the stream the tributaries become so considerable that the beds of most European rivers would fail to contain them. But the mouths of these auxiliary waters Joam Garral and his people will pass as they journey down the Amazon.

To the beauties of this unrivalled river, which waters the finest country in the world, and keeps along its whole course at a few degrees to the south of the equator, there is to be added another quality, possessed by neither the Nile, the Mississippi, nor the Livingstone—or, in other words, the old Congo-Zaira-Lualaba—and that is (although some ill-informed travellers have stated to the contrary) that the Amazon crosses a most healthy part of South America. Its basin is constantly swept by westerly winds. It is not a narrow valley surrounded by high mountains which border its banks, but a huge plain, measuring 350 leagues from north to south, scarcely varied with a few knolls, whose whole extent the atmospheric currents can traverse unchecked.

Professor Agassiz very properly protested against the pretended unhealthiness of the climate of a country which is destined to become one of the most active of the world's producers. According to him, " a soft and gentle breeze is constantly observable, and produces an evaporation, thanks to which the temperature is kept down, and the sun does not give out heat unchecked. The constancy of this refreshing breeze renders the climate of the river Amazon agreeable, and even delightful."

The Abbé Durand has likewise testified that if the temperature does not drop below 25° centigrade, it never rises above 33°, and this gives for the year a mean temperature of from 28° to 29°, with a range of only 8°.

After such statements we are safe in affirming that the basin of the Amazon has none of the burning heats of countries like Asia and Africa, which are crossed by the same parallels.

The vast plain which serves for its valley is accessible over its whole extent to the generous breezes which come from off the Atlantic.

And the provinces to which the river has given its name, have the acknowledged right to call themselves the healthiest of a country which is one of the finest on the earth.

And how can we say that the hydrographical system of the Amazon is not known?

In the sixteenth century Orellana, the lieutenant of one of the brothers Pizarro, descended the Rio Negro, arrived on the main river in 1540, ventured without a guide across the unknown district, and, after eighteen months of a navigation of which his record is most marvellous, reached the mouth.

In 1636 and 1637 the Portuguese Pedro Texeira ascended the Amazon to Napo, with a fleet of forty-seven pirogues.

In 1743 La Condamine, after having measured an arc of the meridian at the equator, left his companions Bouguer and Godin des Odonais, embarked on the Chinchipe, descended it to its junction with the Marañon, reached the mouth at Napo on the 31st of July, just in time to observe an emersion of the first satellite of Jupiter—which allowed this "Humboldt of the eighteenth century" to accurately determine the latitude and longitude of the spot—visited the villages on both banks, and on the 6th of September arrived in front of the fort of Para. This immense journey had important results—not only was the course of the Amazon made out in scientific fashion, but it seemed almost certain that it communicated with the Orinoco.

Fifty-five years later Humboldt and Bonpland completed the valuable work of La Condamine, and drew up the map of the Marañon as far as Napo.

Since this period the Amazon itself and all its principal tributaries have been frequently visited.

In 1827 Lister-Maw, in 1834 and 1835 Smyth, in 1844 the French lieutenant in command of the "Boulonnaise," the Brazilian Valdez in 1840, the French "Paul Marcoy" from 1848 to 1860, the whimsical painter Biard in 1859, Professor Agassiz in 1865 and 1866, in 1867 the Brazilian engineer Franz Keller-Linzenger, and lastly, in 1879 Doctor Crevaux, have explored the course of the river, ascended many of its tributaries, and ascertained the navigability of its principal affluents.

But what has won the greatest honour for the Brazilian Government is that on the 31st July, 1857, after numerous frontier disputes between France and Brazil, about the Guiana boundary, the course of the Amazon was declared to be free and open to all flags ; and, to make practice harmonize with theory, Brazil entered into negotiations with the neighbouring powers for the exploration of every river-road in the basin of the Amazon.

To-day lines of well-found steamboats, which correspond direct with Liverpool, are plying on the river from its mouth up to Manaos; others ascend to Iquitos; others by way of the Tapajoz, the Madiera, the Rio Negro, or

the Purus, make their way into the centre of Peru and
Bolivia.

One can easily imagine the progress which commerce
will one day make in this immense and wealthy area,
which is without a rival in the world.

But to this medal of the future there is a reverse. No
progress can be accomplished without detriment to the
indigenous races.

In fact, on the Upper Amazon many Indian tribes have
already disappeared, amongst others the Curicicurus and
the Sorimaos. On the Putumayo, if a few Yuris are still
met with, the Yahuas have abandoned the district to take
refuge among some of the distant tributaries, and the
Maoos have quitted its banks to wander in their diminished
numbers among the forests of Japura.

The Tunantins is almost depopulated, and there are only
a few families of wandering Indians at the mouth of the
Jurua. The Teffé is almost deserted, and near the sources
of the Japura there remained but the fragments of the
great nation of the Umaüa. The Coari is forsaken. There
are but few Muras Indians on the banks of the Purus.
Of the ancient Manaos one can count but a wandering
party or two. On the banks of the Rio Negro there are
only a few half-breeds, Portuguese and natives, where a few
years ago four-and-twenty different nations had their
homes.

Such is the law of progress. The Indians will disappear. Before the Anglo-Saxon race Australians and Tasmanians have vanished. Before the conquerors of the Far West the North American Indians have been wiped out. One day perhaps the Arabs will be annihilated by the colonization of the French.

But we must return to 1852. The means of communication, so numerous now, did not then exist, and the journey of Joam Garral would require not less than four months, owing to the conditions under which it was made.

Hence this observation of Benito, while the two friends were watching the river as it gently flowed at their feet.

"Manoel, my friend, if there is very little interval between our arrival at Belem and the moment of our separation, the time will appear to you to be very short."

"Yes, Benito," said Manoel, "and very long as well, for Minha cannot be my wife until the end of the voyage."

CHAPTER VI.

A FOREST ON THE GROUND.

THE Garral family were in high glee. The magnificent journey on the Amazon was to be undertaken under conditions as agreeable as possible. Not only were the fazender and his family to start on a voyage for several months, but, as we shall see, he was to be accompanied by a part of the staff of the farm.

In beholding every one happy around him, Joam forgot the anxieties which appeared to trouble his life. From the day his decision was taken he had been another man, and when he busied himself about the preparations for the expedition he regained his former activity. His people rejoiced exceedingly at seeing him again at work. His moral self reacted against his physical self, and Joam again became the active, energetic man of his earlier years, and moved about once more as though he had spent his life in the open air, under the invigorating influences of forests, fields, and running waters.

Moreover, the few weeks that were to precede the departure had been well employed.

At this period, as we have just remarked, the course of the Amazon was not yet furrowed by the numberless steam-vessels, which companies were only then thinking of putting on the river. The service was worked by individuals on their own account alone, and often the boats were only employed in the business of the riverside establishments.

These boats were either "ubas," canoes made from the trunk of a tree, hollowed out by fire, and finished with the axe, pointed and light in front, and heavy and broad in the stern, able to carry from one to a dozen paddlers, and of three or four tons burden: "egariteas," constructed on a larger scale, of broader design, partly covered in the centre with a roof of foliage, and leaving on each side a gangway for the rowers: or, "jangadas," rafts of no particular shape, propelled by a triangular sail, and surmounted by a cabin of mud and straw, which served the Indian and his family for a floating home.

These three kinds of craft formed the lesser flotilla of the Amazon, and were only suited for a moderate traffic of passengers or merchandise.

Larger vessels, however, existed, either "vigilingas," ranging from eight up to ten tons, with three masts rigged with red sails, and which in calm weather were rowed by four long paddles not at all easy to work against the

The larger craft of the Amazon.

stream ; or "cobertas," of twenty tons burthen, a kind of junk with a poop behind and a cabin down below, with two masts and square sails of unequal size, and propelled, when the wind fell, by six long sweeps which Indians worked from a forecastle.

But neither of these vessels satisfied Joam Garral. From the moment that he had resolved to descend the Amazon he had thought of making the most of the voyage by carrying a huge convoy of goods into Para. From this point of view there was no necessity to descend the river in a hurry. And the determination to which he had come pleased every one, excepting, perhaps, Manoel, who would for very good reasons have preferred some rapid steamboat.

But though the means of transport devised by Joam were primitive in the extreme, he was going to take with him a numerous following and abandon himself to the stream under exceptional conditions of comfort and security.

It would be, in truth, as if a part of the fazenda of Iquitos had been cut away from the bank and carried down the Amazon with all that composed the family of the fazender—masters and servants, in their dwellings, their cottages, and their huts.

The settlement of Iquitos included a part of those magnificent forests which, in the central districts of South America, are practically inexhaustible.

F

Joam Garral thoroughly understood the management of these woods, which were rich in the most precious and diverse species adapted for joinery, cabinet work, ship-building, and carpentry, and from them he annually drew considerable profits.

The river was there in front of him, and could it not be as safely and economically used as a railway if one existed? So every year Joam Garral felled some hundreds of trees from his stock and formed immense rafts of floating wood, of joists, beams, and slightly squared trunks, which were taken to Para in charge of capable pilots who were thoroughly acquainted with the depths of the river and the direction of its currents.

This year Joam Garral decided to do as he had done in preceding years. Only, when the raft was made up, he was going to leave to Benito all the detail of the trading part of the business. But there was no time to lose. The beginning of June was the best season to start for the waters increased by the floods of the upper basin would gradually and gradually subside until the month of October.

The first steps had thus to be taken without delay, for the raft was to be of unusual proportions. It would be necessary to fell a half-mile square of the forest which was situated at the junction of the Nanay and the Amazon —that is to say, the whole river side of the fazenda, to form the enormous mass, for such were the jangadas, or river rafts, which attained the dimensions of a small island.

It was in this jangada, safer than any other vessel of the country, larger than a hundred egariteas or vigilingas coupled together, that Joam Garral proposed to embark with his family, his servants, and his merchandise.

"Excellent idea!" had cried Minha, clapping her hands, when she learnt her father's scheme.

"Yes," said Yaquita, "and in that way we shall reach Belem without danger or fatigue."

"And during the stoppages we can have some hunting in the forests on the banks," added Benito.

"Won't it take rather long?" observed Manoel; "could we not hit upon some quicker way of descending the Amazon?"

It would take some time, obviously, but the interested observation of the young doctor received no attention from any one.

Joam Garral then called in an Indian who was the principal manager of the fazenda.

"In a month," he said to him, "the jangada must be built and ready to launch!"

"We'll set to work this very day, sir!"

It was a heavy task. There were about a hundred Indians and blacks, and during the first fortnight in May they did wonders. Some people unaccustomed to these great tree-massacres, would perhaps have groaned to see giants many hundred years old fall in a few hours beneath the axes of the woodmen; but there was such a quantity on the banks of the river, up stream and down stream, even to the most distant points of the horizon, that the felling of this half-mile of forest would scarcely leave an appreciable void.

The superintendent of the men, after receiving the instructions of Joam Garral, had first cleared the ground of the creepers, brushwood, weeds, and arborescent plants which obstructed it. Before taking to the saw and the axe they had armed themselves with a felling-sword, that indispensable tool of every one who desires to penetrate the Amazonian forests, a large blade slightly curved, wide and flat, and two or three feet long, and strongly handled, which the natives wield with consummate address. In a few hours, with the help of the felling-sword, they had cleared the ground, cut down the underwood, and opened large gaps into the densest portions of the wood.

In this way the work progressed. The ground was cleared in front of the woodmen. The old trunks were divested of their clothing of creepers, cacti, ferns, mosses, and bromelias. They were stripped naked to the bark, until such time as the bark itself was stripped from off them.

Among the trees.

Page 69.

The felling of the forest.

Then the whole of the workers, before whom fled an innumerable crowd of monkeys who were hardly their superiors in agility, slung themselves into the upper branches, sawing off the heavier boughs and cutting down the topmost limbs, which had to be cleared away on the spot. Very soon there remained only a doomed forest, with long bare stems, bereft of their crowns, through which the sun luxuriantly shot its rays on to the humid soil which perhaps it had never before caressed.

There was not a single tree which could not be used for some work of skill, either in carpentry or cabinet-work. There, shooting up like columns of ivory ringed with brown, were wax-palms 120 feet high, and four feet thick at their base ; white chestnuts, which yield the three-cornered nuts ; "murichis," unexcelled for building purposes ; "barrigudos," measuring a couple of yards at the swelling, which is found at a few feet above the earth, trees with shining russet bark dotted with grey tubercles, each pointed stem of which supports a horizontal parasol ; and "bombax" of superb stature, with its straight and smooth white stem. Amongst these magnificent specimens of the Amazonian flora there fell many "quatibos," whose rosy canopies towered above the neighbouring trees, whose fruits are like little cups with rows of chestnuts ranged within, and whose wood of clear violet is specially in demand for ship-building And besides there was the iron wood, and more particularly

the "ibiriratea," nearly black in its skin, and so close
grained that of it the Indians make their battle-axes;
"jacarandas," more precious than mahogany; "cæsal-
pinas," only now found in the depths of the old forests
which have escaped the woodman's axe; "sapucaias," 150
feet high, buttressed by natural arches, which, starting
from three yards from their base, rejoin the tree some
thirty feet up the stem, twining themselves round the trunk
like the filatures of a twisted column, whose head expands
in a bouquet of vegetable fireworks made up of the yellow,
purple, and snowy white of the parasitic plants.

Three weeks after the work was begun not one was
standing of all the trees which had covered the angle of
the Amazon and the Nanay. The clearance was complete. Joam Garral had not even had to bestir himself in
the demolition of a forest which it would take twenty or
thirty years to replace. Not a stick of young or old wood
was left to mark the boundary of a future clearing, not even
an angle to mark the limit of the denudation. It was indeed
a clean sweep; the trees were cut to the level of the earth,
to wait the day when their roots would be got out, over
which the coming spring would still spread its verdant
cloak.

This square space, washed on its sides by the waters of
the river and its tributary, was destined to be cleared,
ploughed, planted, and sown, and the following year fields

of manioc, coffee-shrubs, sugar-canes, arrowroot, maize, and pea-nuts would occupy the ground so recently covered by the trees.

The last week of the month had not arrived when the trunks, classified according to their varieties and specific gravity, were symmetrically arranged on the bank of the Amazon, at the spot where the immense jangada was to be built—which, with the different habitations for the accommodation of the crew, would become a veritable floating village—to wait the time when the waters of the river, swollen by the floods, would raise it and carry it for hundreds of leagues to the Atlantic coast.

The whole time the work was going on Joam Garral had been engaged in superintending it. From the clearing to the bank of the fazenda he had formed a large mound on which the portions of the raft were disposed, and to this matter he had attended entirely himself.

Yaquita was occupied with Cybele with the preparations ·for the departure, though the old negress could not be made to understand why they wanted to go or what they hoped to see.

"But you will see things that you never saw before," Yaquita kept saying to her.

"Will they be better than what we see now?" was Cybele's invariable reply.

Minha and her favourite for their part took care of what

more particularly concerned them. They were not preparing for a simple voyage ; for them it was a permanent
departure, and there were a thousand details to look after
for settling in the other country in which the young mulatto
was to live with the mistress to whom she was so devotedly
attached. Minha was a trifle sorrowful, but the joyous
Lina was quite unaffected at leaving Iquitos. Minha Valdez
would be the same to her as Minha Garral, and to check
her spirits she would have to be separated from her mistress, and that was never thought of.

Benito had actively assisted his father in the work, which
was on the point of completion. He commenced his
apprenticeship to the trade of a fazender, which would probably one day become his own, as he was about to do to
that of a merchant on their descent of the river.

As for Manoel, he divided his time between the house,
where Yaquita and her daughter were as busy as possible,
and the clearing, to which Benito fetched him rather oftener
than he thought convenient, and on the whole the division
was very unequal, as may well be imagined.

CHAPTER VII.

FOLLOWING A LIANA.

IT was a Sunday, the 26th of May, and the young people had made up their minds to take a holiday. The weather was splendid, the heat being tempered by the refreshing breezes which blew from off the Cordilleras, and everything invited them out for an excursion into the country.

Benito and Manoel had offered to accompany Minha through the thick woods which bordered the right bank of the Amazon opposite the fazenda.

It was, in a manner, a farewell visit to the charming environs of Iquitos. The young men went equipped for the chase, but as sportsmen who had no intention of going far from their companions in pursuit of any game. Manoel could be trusted for that, and the girls—for Lina could not leave her mistress—went prepared for a walk, an excursion of two or three leagues being not too long to frighten them.

Neither Joam Garral nor Yaquita had time to go with

them. For one reason the plan of the jangada was not yet complete, and it was necessary that its construction should not be interrupted for a day, and another was that Yaquita and Cybele, well seconded as they were by the domestics of the fazenda, had not an hour to lose.

Minha had accepted the offer with much pleasure, and so, after breakfast on the day we speak of, at about eleven o'clock, the two young men and the two girls met on the bank at the angle were the two streams joined. One of the blacks went with them. They all embarked in one of the ubas used in the service of the farm, and after having passed between the islands of Iquitos and Parianta, they reached the right bank of the Amazon.

They landed at a clump of superb tree-ferns, which were crowned, at a height of some thirty feet, with a sort of halo made of the dainty branches of green velvet and the delicate lacework of the drooping fronds.

"Well, Manoel," said Minha, "it is for me to do the honours of the forest, you are only a stranger in these regions of the Upper Amazon! We are at home here, and you must allow me to do my duty, as mistress of the house."

"Dearest Minha!" replied the young man, "you will be none the less mistress of your house in our town of Belem, than at the fazenda of Iquitos, and there as here—"

"Now then!" interrupted Benito, "you did not come

The farewell ramble.

Page 74.

here to exchange loving speeches, I imagine ! Just forget
for a few hours that you are engaged ! "

" Not for an hour—not for an instant ! " said Manoel.

" Perhaps you will if Minha orders you ? "

" Minha will not order me."

" Who knows ? " said Lina, laughing.

" Lina is right," answered Minha, who held out her
hand to Manoel. " Try to forget ! Forget ! my brother
requires it. All is broken off ! As long as this walk
lasts we are not engaged : I am no more than the sister
of Benito ! You are only my friend ! "

" To be sure," said Benito.

" Bravo ! Bravo ! there are only strangers here," said the
young mulatto, clapping her hands.

" Strangers who see each other for the first time," added
the girl ; " who meet, bow to—"

" Mademoiselle ! " said Manoel, turning to Minha.

" To whom have I the honour to speak, sir ? " said she
in the most serious manner possible.

" To Manoel Valdez, who will be glad if your brother
will introduce me."

" Oh, away with your nonsense ! " cried Benito. " Stupid
idea that I had ! Be engaged, my friends—be it as much
as you like ! Be it always ! "

" Always ! " said Minha, from whom the word escaped
so naturally that Lina's peals of laughter redoubled.

A grateful glance from Manoel repaid Minha for the imprudence of her tongue.

"Come along," said Benito, so as to get his sister out of her embarrassment; "if we walk on we shall not talk so much."

"One moment, brother," she said. "You have seen how ready I am to obey you. You wished to oblige Manoel and me to forget each other, so as not to spoil your walk. Very well; and now I am going to ask a sacrifice from you so that you shall not spoil mine. Whether it pleases you or not, Benito, you must promise me to forget—"

"Forget what?"

"That you are a sportsman!"

"What! you forbid me to—"

"I forbid you to fire at any of these charming birds—any of the parrots, caciques, or curucus which are flying about so happily among the trees! And the same interdiction with regard to the smaller game with which we shall have to do to-day. If any ounce, jaguar, or such thing comes too near, well—"

"But—" said Benito.

"If not, I will take Manoel's arm, and we shall save or lose ourselves, and you will be obliged to run after us!"

"Would you not like me to refuse, eh?" asked Benito, looking at Manoel.

"I think I should!" replied the young man.

"Well, then—no!" said Benito; "I do not refuse; I will obey and annoy you. Come on!"

And so the four, followed by the black, struck under the splendid trees, whose thick foliage prevented the sun's rays from ever reaching the soil.

There is nothing more magnificent than this part of the right bank of the Amazon. There, in such picturesque confusion, so many different trees shoot up that it is possible to count more than a hundred different species in a square mile. A forester could easily see that no woodman had been there with his hatchet or axe, for the effects of a clearing are visible for many centuries afterwards. If the new trees are even a hundred years old, the general aspect still differs from what it was originally, for the lianas and other parasitic plants alter, and signs remain which no native can misunderstand.

The happy group moved then into the tall herbage, across the thickets and under the bushes, chatting and laughing. In front, when the brambles were too thick, the negro, felling-sword in hand, cleared the way, and put thousands of birds to flight.

Minha was right to intercede for the little winged world which flew about in the higher foliage, for the finest representations of tropical ornithology were there to be seen —green parrots and clamorous parrakeets, which seemed to be the natural fruit of these gigantic trees; hummingbirds in all their varieties, light-blue and ruby red; "tis-auras" with long scissors-like tails, looking like detached flowers, which the wind blew from branch to branch; blackbirds, with orange plumage bound with brown; golden-edged beccaficos; and "sabias," black as crows; all united in a deafening concert of shrieks and whistles. The long beak of the toucan stood out against the golden clusters of the "quiriris," and the treepeckers or wood-peckers of Brazil wagged their little heads, speckled all over with their purple spots. It was truly a scene of en-chantment.

But all were silent and went into hiding when above the tops of the trees there grated like a rusty weathercock the "alma de gato" or "soul of the cat," a kind of light fawn-coloured sparrow-hawk. If he proudly hooted, displaying in the air the long white plumes of his tail, he in his turn meekly took to flight when in the loftier heights there appeared the "gaviao," the large white-headed eagle, the terror of the whole winged population of these woods.

Minha made Manoel admire the natural wonders which could not be found in their simplicity in the more civi-lized provinces of the east. He listened to her more with his eyes than his ears, for the cries and the songs of these thousands of birds were every now and then so penetrat-ing that he was not able to hear what she said. The noisy laughter of Lina was alone sufficiently shrill to ring out with its joyous note above every kind of clucking, chirping, hooting, whistling, and cooing.

At the end of an hour they had scarcely gone a mile. As they left the river the trees assumed another aspect, and the animal life was no longer met with near the ground, but at from sixty to eighty feet above, where troops of monkeys chased each other along the higher branches. Here and there a few cones of the solar rays shot down into the underwood. In fact in these tropical forests light does not seem to be necessary for their existence. The air is enough for the vegetable growth, whether it be large or small, tree or plant, and all the heat required for the development of their sap is derived not from the surrounding atmosphere, but from the bosom of the soil itself, where it is stored up as in an enormous stove.

And on the bromelias, grass-plantains, orchids, cacti, and in short all the parasites which formed a little forest beneath the large one, many marvellous insects were they tempted to pluck as though they had been genuine blossoms— nestors with blue wings like shimmering watered silk, leilu butterflies reflexed with gold and striped with fringes of green, agrippina moths, ten inches long, with leaves for wings, maribunda bees, like living emeralds set in sockets of gold, and legions of lampyrons or pyrophorus coleopters, valagumas with breastplates of bronze, and green elytræ, with yellow light pouring from their eyes, who, when the night comes, illuminate the forest with their many-coloured scintillations.

"What wonders!" repeated the enthusiastic girl.

"You are at home, Minha, or at least you say so," said Benito, "and that is the way you talk of your riches!"

"Sneer away, little brother!" replied Minha; "such beautiful things are only lent to us; is it not so, Manoel? They come from the hand of the Almighty and belong to the world!"

"Let Benito laugh on, Minha," said Manoel. "He hides it very well, but he is a poet himself when his time comes, and he admires as much as we do all these beauties of nature. Only when his gun is on his arm, good-bye to poetry!"

"Then be a poet now," replied the girl.

"I am a poet," said Benito. "O! Nature-enchanting, etc."

We may confess, however, that in forbidding him to use his gun Minha had imposed on him a genuine privation. There was no lack of game in the woods, and several magnificent opportunities he had declined with regret.

In some of the less wooded parts, in places where the breaks were tolerably spacious, they saw several pairs of ostriches, of the species known as "naudus," from four to five feet high, accompanied by their inseparable "seriemas," a sort of turkey, infinitely better from an edible point of view than the huge birds they escort.

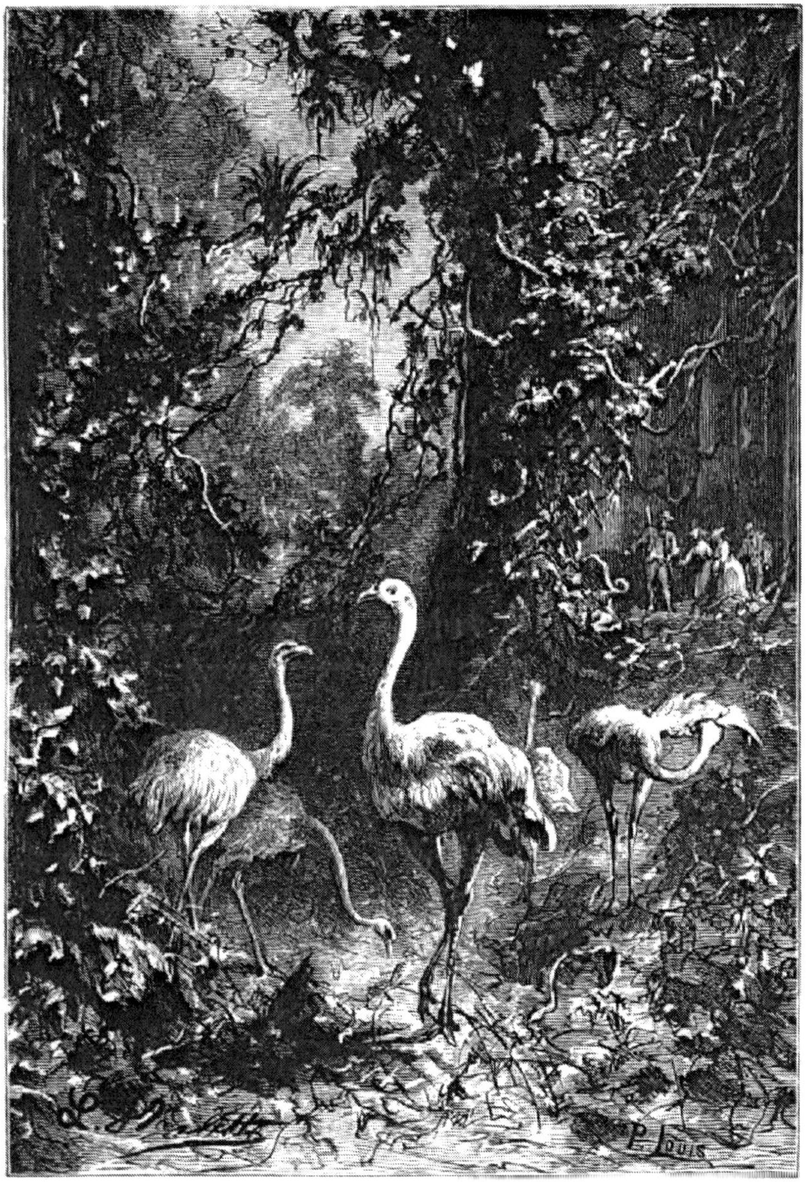
P. Louis

The Naudus.

Page 80.

"See what that wretched promise costs me!" sighed Benito, as, at a gesture from his sister, he replaced under his arm the gun which had instinctively gone up to his shoulder.

"We ought to respect the seriemas," said Manoel, "for they are great destroyers of the snakes."

"Just as we ought to respect the snakes," replied Benito, "because they eat the noxious insects, and just as we ought the insects because they live on smaller insects more offensive still! At that rate we ought to respect everything."

But the instinct of the young sportsman was about to be put to a still more rigorous trial. The woods became of a sudden full of game. Swift stags and graceful roebucks scampered off beneath the bushes, and a well aimed bullet would assuredly have stopped them. Here and there turkeys showed themselves with their milk and coffee coloured plumage: and peccaries, a sort of wild pig highly appreciated by lovers of venison, and agouties, which are the hares and rabbits of Central America; and tatous belonging to the order of edentates, with their scaly shells of patterns of mosaic.

And truly Benito showed more than virtue, and even genuine heroism, when he came across some tapirs called "antas" in Brazil, diminutives of the elephant, already nearly undiscoverable on the banks of the Upper Amazon and its tributaries, pachyderms so dear to the hunters for

G

their rarity, so appreciated by gourmands for their meat, superior far to beef, and above all for the protuberance on the nape of the neck, which is a morsel fit for a king !

His gun almost burnt his fingers, but faithful to his promise, he kept it quiet.

But yet—and he cautioned his sister about this—the gun would go off in spite of him, and probably register a master-stroke in sporting annals, if within range there should come a " tamandqa assa," a kind of large and very curious ant-eater.

Happily the big ant-eater did not show himself, neither did any panthers, leopards, jaguars, guepars, or conguars, called indifferently ounces in South America, and to whom it is not advisable to get too near.

"After all," said Benito, who stopped for an instant, "to walk is very well, but to walk without an object—"

"Without an object!" replied his sister; "but our object is to see, to admire, to visit for the last time these forests of Central America, which we shall not find again in Para, and to bid them a last farewell ! "

"Ah ! an idea ! "

It was Lina who spoke.

"An idea of Lina's can be no other than a silly one !" said Benito, shaking his head.

"It is unkind, brother," said Minha, " to make fun of

Lina when she has been thinking how to give our walk the object which you have just regretted it lacks."

" Besides, Mr. Benito, I am sure my idea will please you,', replied the mulatto.

" Well, what is it ? " asked Minha.

" You see that liana ? "

And Lina pointed to a liana of the "cipos" kind, twisted round a gigantic sensitive mimosa, whose leaves, light as feathers, shut up at the least disturbance.

" Well ? " said Benito.

" I propose," replied Minha, "that we try to follow that liana to its very end."

" It is an idea, and it is an object!" observed Benito, "to follow this liana, no matter what may be the obstacles thickets, underwood, rocks, brooks, torrents, to let nothing stop us, not even—"

" Certainly, you are right, brother !" said Minha ; " Lina is a trifle absurd."

" Come on, then!" replied her brother; "you say that Lina is absurd so as to say that Benito is absurd to approve of it ! "

" Well, both of you are absurd, if that will amuse you," returned Minha.   " Let us follow the liana !"

" You are not afraid ? " said Manoel.

" Still objections !" shouted Benito.

" Ah, Manoel ! you would not speak like that if you

were already on your way and Minha was waiting for you at the end."

·" I am silent," replied Manoel ; "I have no more to say. I obey. Let us follow the liana!"

And off they went as happy as children home for their holidays.

This vegetable might take them far if they determined to follow it to its extremity, like the thread of Ariadne, as far almost as that which the heiress of Minos used to lead her from the labyrinth, and perhaps entangle them more deeply.

· It was in fact a creeper of the salses family, one of the cipos known under the name of the red "japicanga," whose length sometimes measures several miles. But, after all, they could leave it when they liked.

The cipo passed from one tree to another without breaking its continuity, sometimes twisting round the trunks, sometimes garlanding the branches, here jumping from a dragon-tree to a rosewood, then from a gigantic chestnut, the "Bertholletia excelsa," to some of the wine palms, "baccabas," whose branches have been appropriately compared by Agassiz to long sticks of coral flecked with green. Here round "tucumas," or ficuses, capriciously twisted like centenarian olive-trees, and of which Brazil has fifty-four varieties ; here round the kinds of euphorbias, which produce caoutchouc, "gualtes," noble palm-trees, with slender, graceful, and glossy stems ; and cacao-trees, which shoot up of their own accord on the banks of the Amazon and its tributaries, having different melastomas, some with red flowers and others ornamented with panicles of whitish berries.

But the halts! the shouts of cheating! when the happy company thought they had lost their guiding thread! For it was necessary to go back and disentangle it from the knot of parasitic plants.

"There it is!" said Lina, "I see it!"

"You are wrong," replied Minha; "that is not it, that is a liana of another kind."

"No, Lina is right!" said Benito.

"No, Lina is wrong!" Manoel would naturally return.

Hence highly serious, long-continued discussions, in which no one would give in.

Then the black on one side and Benito on the other would rush at the trees and clamber up to the branches encircled by the cipo so as to arrive at the true direction.

Now nothing was assuredly less easy in that jumble of knots, among which twisted the liana in the middle of bromelias, "karatas," armed with their sharp prickles, orchids with rosy flowers and violet lips of the size of gloves, and oncidiums more tangled than a skein of worsted between a kitten's paws.

And then when the liana ran down again to the ground the difficulty of picking it out under the mass of lycopods, large-leaved heliconias, rosy-tasselled calliandras, rhipsalas encircling it like the thread on an electric reel, between the knots of the large white ipomas, under the fleshy stems of the vanilla, and in the midst of the shoots and branchlets of the grenadilla and the vine.

And when the cipo was found again what shouts of joy, and how they resumed the walk for an instant interrupted !

For an hour the young people had already been advancing, and nothing had happened to warn them that they were approaching the end.

They shook the liana with vigour, but it would not give and the birds flew away in hundreds, and the monkeys fled from tree to tree, so as to point out the way.

If a thicket barred the road the felling-sword cut a deep gap, and the group passed in. If it was a high rock, carpeted with verdure, over which the liana twined like a serpent, they climbed it and passed on.

A large break now appeared. There, in the more open air, which is as necessary to it as the light of the sun, the tree of the tropics, *par excellence*, which, according to Humboldt, "accompanies man in the infancy of his civilization," the great provider of the inhabitant of the torrid zones, a banana-tree, was standing alone. The long festoon of the liana curled round its higher branches, moving away to the other side of the clearing, and disappeared again into the forest.

"Shall we stop soon?" asked Manoel.

"No; a thousand times no!" cried Benito, "not without having reached the end of it!"

"Perhaps," observed Minha, "it will soon be time to think of returning."

"Oh, dearest mistress, let us go on again!" replied Lina.

"On for ever!" added Benito.

And they plunged more deeply into the forest, which, becoming clearer, allowed them to advance more easily.

Besides, the cipo bore away to the north, and towards the river. It became less inconvenient to follow seeing that they approached the right bank, and it would be easy to get back afterwards.

A quarter of an hour later they all stopped at the foot of a ravine in front of a small tributary of the Amazon. But a bridge of lianas, made of "bejucos," twined together by their interlacing branches, crossed the stream. The cipo, dividing into two strings, served for a handrail, and passed from one bank to the other.

Benito, all the time in front, had already stepped on the swinging floor of this vegetable bridge.

Manoel wished to keep his sister back.

"Stay—stay, Minha!" he said, "Benito may go farther if he likes, but let us remain here."

"No! Come on, come on, dear mistress!" cried Lina,

"Don't be afraid, the liana is getting thinner; we shall get the better of it, and find out its end!"

And, without hesitation, the young mulatto boldly ventured behind Benito.

"What children they are!" replied Minha. "Come along, Manoel, we must follow."

And they all cleared the bridge, which swayed above the ravine like a swing, and plunged again beneath the mighty trees.

But they had not proceeded for ten minutes along the interminable cipo, in the direction of the river, when they stopped, and this time not without cause.

"Have we got to the end of this liana?" asked Minha.

"No," replied Benito; "but we had better advance with care. Look!" and Benito pointed to the cipo which, lost in the branches of a high ficus, was agitated by violent shakings.

"What causes that?" asked Manoel.

"Perhaps some animal that we had better approach with a little circumspection!"

And Benito, cocking his gun, motioned them to let him go on a bit, and stepped about ten paces to the front.

Manoel, the two girls, and the black remained motionless where they were.

Suddenly Benito raised a shout, and they saw him rush towards a tree; they all ran as well.

The cipo bridge.

Page 88.

Sight the most unforeseen, and little adapted to gratify the eyes!

A man, hanging by the neck, struggled at the end of the liana, which, supple as a cord, had formed into a slipknot, and the shakings came from the jerks into which he still agitated it in the last convulsions of his agony!

Benito threw himself on the unfortunate fellow, and with a cut of his hunting-knife severed the cipo.

The man slipped on to the ground. Manoel leant over him, to try and recall him to life, if it was not too late.

"Poor man!" murmured Minha.

"Mr. Manoel! Mr. Manoel!" cried Lina. "He breathes again! His heart beats; you must save him."

"True," said Manoel, "but I think it was about time that we came up."

He was about thirty years old, a white, clothed badly enough, much emaciated, and he seemed to have suffered a good deal.

At his feet were an empty flask, thrown on the ground, and a cup and ball in palm wood, of which the ball, made of the head of a tortoise, was tied on with a fibre.

"To hang himself! to hang himself!" repeated Lina, "and young still! What could have driven him to do such a thing?"

But the attempts of Manoel had not been long in bring-

ing the luckless wight to life again, and he opened his eyes
and gave an "ahem!" so vigorous and unexpected, that
Lina, frightened, replied to his cry with another.

"Who are you, my friend?" Benito asked him.

"An ex-hanger-on, as far as I see."

"But your name?"

"Wait a minute and I will recall myself," said he, passing his hand over his forehead. "I am known as Fragoso,
at your service; and I am still able to curl and cut your
hair, to shave you, and to make you comfortable according
to all the rules of my art. I am a barber, so to speak more
truly, the most desperate of Figaros."

"And what made you think of—"

"What would you have, my gallant sir?" replied
Fragoso, with a smile; "a moment of despair, which I
would have duly regretted had the regrets been in another
world! But 800 leagues of country to traverse, and not a
coin in my pouch, was not very comforting! I had lost
courage obviously."

To conclude, Fragoso had a good and pleasing figure,
and as he recovered it was evident that he was of a lively
disposition. He was one of those wandering barbers who
travel on the banks of the Upper Amazon, going from
village to village, and putting the resources of their art at
the service of negroes, negresses, Indians, and Indian
women, who appreciate them very much,

The finding of Fragoso.

Page 90.

But poor Fragoso, abandoned and miserable, having eaten nothing for forty hours, astray in the forest, had for an instant lost his head, and we know the rest.

"My friend," said Benito to him, "you will go back with us to the fazenda of Iquitos?"

"With pleasure," replied Fragoso; "you cut me down, and I belong to you. I must somehow be dependent."

"Well, dear mistress, don't you think we did well to continue our walk?" asked Lina.

"That I do!" returned the girl.

"Never mind," said Benito; "I never thought that we should finish by finding a man at the end of the cipo."

"And, above all, a barber in difficulties, and on the road to hang himself!" replied Fragoso.

The poor fellow, who was now wide awake, was told about what had passed. He warmly thanked Lina for the good idea she had had of following the liana, and they all started on the road to the fazenda, where Fragoso was received in a way that gave him neither wish nor want to try his wretched task again.

CHAPTER VIII.

THE JANGADA.

THE half-mile square of forest was cleared. With the car-
penters remained the task of arranging in the form of a
raft the many venerable trees which were lying on the strand.

And an easy task it was!   Under the direction of Joam
Garral the Indians displayed their incomparable ingenuity.
In everything connected with house-building or ship-building these natives are, it must be admitted, astonishing
workmen. They have only an axe and a saw, and they
work on woods so hard that the edge of their tools gets
absolutely jagged; yet they square up trunks, shape beams
out of enormous stems, and get out of them joists and
planking without the aid of any machinery whatever, and,
endowed with prodigious natural ability, do all these things
easily with their skilled and patient hands.

The trees had not been launched into the Amazon to
begin with; Joam Garral was accustomed to proceed in a
different way. The whole mass of trunks was symmetri-

cally arranged on a flat part of the bank, which he had already levelled up at the junction of the Nanay with the great river.

There it was that the jangada was to be built ; thence it was that the Amazon was to float it when the time came for it to start for its destination.

And here an explanatory note is necessary in regard to the geography of this immense body of water, and more especially as relating to a singular phenomenon which the river-side inhabitants describe from personal observation.

The two rivers which are, perhaps, more extensive than the great artery of Brazil, the Nile and the Missouri-Mississippi, flow one from south to north across the African continent, the other from north to south through North America. They cross districts of many different latitudes, and consequently of many different climates.

The Amazon, on the contrary, is entirely comprised—at least, it is from the point where it turns to the east, on the frontiers of Ecuador and Peru—between the second and fourth parallels of south latitude. Hence this immense river-system is under the same climatic conditions during the whole of its course.

In these parts there are two distinct seasons during which the rain falls. In the north of Brazil the rainy season is in September ; in the south it occurs in March. Consequently the right-hand tributaries and the left-hand tributaries bring down their floods at half-yearly intervals, and hence the level of the Amazon, after reaching its maximum in June, gradually falls until October.

This Joam Garral knew by experience, and he intended to profit by the phenomenon to launch the jangada, after having built it in comfort on the river-bank. In fact, between the mean and the higher level the height of the Amazon could vary as much as forty feet, and between the mean and the lower level as much as thirty feet. A difference of seventy feet like this gave the fazender all he required.

The building was commenced without delay. Along the huge bank the trunks were got into place according to their sizes and floating power, which of course had to be taken into account, as among these thick and heavy woods there were many whose specific gravity was but little below that of water.

The first layer was entirely composed of trunks laid side by side. A little interval had to be left between them, and they were bound together by transverse beams, which assured the solidity of the whole. " Piaçaba " ropes strapped them together as firmly as any chain cables could have done. This material, which consists of the ramicles of a certain palm-tree growing very abundantly on the river-banks, is in universal use in the district. Piaçaba floats, resists immersion, and is cheaply made—very good

Building the raft.

Page 94.

reasons for causing it to be valuable, and making it even an article of commerce with the Old World.

Above this double row of trunks and beams were disposed the joists and planks which formed the floor of the jangada, and rose about thirty inches above the load water-line. The bulk was enormous, as we must confess when it is considered that the raft measured a thousand feet long and sixty broad, and thus had a superficies of sixty thousand square feet. They were, in fact, about to commit a whole forest to the Amazon.

The work of building was conducted under the immediate direction of Joam Garral. But when that part was finished the question of arrangement was submitted to the discussion of all, including even the gallant Fragoso.

Just a word as to what he was doing in his new situation at the fazenda.

The barber had never been so happy as since the day when he had been received by the hospitable family. Joam Garral had offered to take him to Para, on the road to which he was when the liana, according to his account, had seized him by the neck and brought him up with a round turn. Fragoso had accepted the offer, thanked him from the bottom of his heart, and ever since had sought to make himself useful in a thousand ways. He was a very intelligent fellow—what one might call a "double right-hander" —that is to say, he could do everything, and could do everything well. As merry as Lina, always singing, and always ready with some good-natured joke, he was not long in being liked by all.

But it was with the young mulatto that he claimed to have contracted the heaviest obligation.

"A famous idea that of yours, Miss Lina," he was constantly saying, "to play at 'following the liana!' It is a capital game even if you do not always find a poor chap of a barber at the end!"

"Quite a chance, Mr. Fragoso," would laughingly reply Lina; "I assure you, you owe me nothing!"

"What! nothing! I owe you my life, and I want it prolonged for a hundred years, and that my recollection of the fact may endure even longer! You see, it is not my trade to be hanged! If I tried my hand at it, it was through necessity. But, on consideration, I would rather die of hunger, and before quite going off I should try a little pasturage with the brutes! As for this liana, it is a lien between us, and so you will see!"

The conversation generally took a joking turn, but at the bottom Fragoso was very grateful to the mulatto for having taken the initiative in his rescue, and Lina was not insensible to the attentions of the brave fellow, who was as straightforward, frank, and good-looking as she was. Their friendship gave rise to many a pleasant "Ah, ah!" on the part of Benito, old Cybele, and others.

To return to the jangada. After some discussion it was decided, as the voyage was to be of some months' duration, to make it as complete and comfortable as possible. The Garral family, comprising the father, mother, daughter, Benito, Manoel, and the servants, Cybele and Lina, were to live in a separate house. In addition to these, there were to go forty Indians, forty blacks, Fragoso, and the pilot who was to take charge of the navigation of the raft.

Though the crew was large, it was not more than sufficient for the service on board. To work the jangada along the windings of the river and between the hundreds of islands and islets which lay in its course required fully as many as were taken, for if the current furnished the motive power, it had nothing to do with the steering, and the hundred and sixty arms were no more than were necessary to work the long boat-hooks by which the giant raft was to be kept in mid-stream.

In the first place, then, in the hinder part of the jangada they built the master's house. It was arranged to contain several bedrooms and a large dining-hall. One of the rooms was destined for Joam and his wife, another for Lina and Cybele near those of their mistresses, and a third room for Benito and Manoel. Minha had a room away from the others, which was not by any means the least comfortably designed.

This, the principal house, was carefully made of weather-

H

boarding, saturated with boiling resin, and thus rendered water-tight throughout. It was capitally lighted with windows on all sides. In front, the entrance-door gave immediate access to the common room. A light verandah, resting on slender bamboos, protected the exterior from the direct action of the solar rays. The whole was painted a light-ochre colour, which reflected the heat instead of absorbing it, and kept down the temperature of the interior.

But when the heavy work, so to speak, had been completed, Minha intervened with,—

" Father, now your care has enclosed and covered us, you must allow us to arrange our dwelling to please ourselves. The outside belongs to you, the inside to us. Mother and I would like it to be as though our house at the fazenda went with us on the journey, so as to make you fancy that we had never left Iquitos !"

" Do just as you like, Minha," replied Joam Garral, smiling in the sad way he often did.

" That will be nice ! "

" I leave everything to your good taste."

" And that will do us honour, father. It ought to, for the sake of the splendid country we are going through— which is yours, by-the-way, and into which you are to enter after so many years' absence."

" Yes, Minha ; yes," replied Joam. " It is rather as if

we were returning from exile—voluntary exile! Do your best; I approve beforehand of what you do."

On Minha and Lina, to whom were added of their own free will Manoel on the one side and Fragoso on the other, devolved the care of decorating the inside of the house. With some imagination and a little artistic feeling the result was highly satisfactory.

The best furniture of the fazenda naturally found its place within, as after arriving in Para they could easily return it by one of the igariteas. Tables, bamboo easy-chairs, cane sofas, carved wood shelves, everything that constituted the charming furniture of the tropics, was disposed with taste about the floating house. No one is likely to imagine that the walls remained bare. The boards were hidden beneath hangings of most agreeable variety. These hangings were made of valuable bark, that of the "tuturis," which is raised up in large folds like the brocades and damasks and softest and richest materials of our modern looms. On the floors of the rooms were jaguar skins, with wonderful spots, and thick monkey furs of exquisite fleeciness. Light curtains of the russet silk, produced by the "suma-uma," hung from the windows. The beds, enveloped in mosquito curtains, had their pillows, mattresses, and bolsters filled with that fresh and elastic substance which in the Upper Amazon is yielded by the bombax.

Throughout on the shelves and side-tables were little
odds and ends, brought from Rio Janeiro or Belem, those
most precious to Minha being such as had come from
Manoel. What could be more pleasing in her eyes than
the nicknacks given by a loving hand which spoke to her
without saying anything?

In a few days the interior was completed, and it looked
just like the interior of the fazenda. A stationary house
under a lovely clump of trees on the borders of some beautiful river! Until it descended between the banks of the
larger stream it would not be out of keeping with the
picturesque landscape which stretched away on each side
of it.

We may add that the exterior of the house was no less
charming than the interior.

In fact, on the outside the young fellows had given free
scope to their taste and imagination.

From the basement to the roof it was literally covered
with foliage. A confused mass of orchids, bromelias, and
climbing plants, all in flower, rooted in boxes of excellent
soil hidden beneath masses of verdure. The trunk of some
ficus or mimosa was never covered by a more startlingly
tropical attire. What whimsical climbers—ruby red and
golden yellow, with variegated clusters and tangled twigs—
turned over the brackets, under the ridges, on the rafters
of the roof, and across the lintels of the doors! They had

brought them wholesale from the woods in the neighbour-hood of the fazenda. A huge liana bound all the parasites together; several times it made the round of the house, clinging on to every angle, encircling every projection, forking, uniting, it everywhere threw out its irregular branchlets, and allowed not a bit of the house to be seen beneath its enormous clusters of bloom.

As a delicate piece of attention, the author of which can be easily recognized, the end of the cipo spread out before the very window of the young mulatto, as though a long arm was for ever holding a bouquet of fresh flowers across the blind.

To sum up, it was as charming as could be; and as Yaquita, her daughter, and Lina were content, we need say no more about it.

"It would not take much to make us plant trees on the jangada," said Benito.

"Oh, trees!" ejaculated Minha.

"Why not?" replied Manoel. "Transported on to this solid platform, with some good soil, I am sure they would do well, and we would have no change of climate to fear for them, as the Amazon flows all the time along the same parallel."

"Besides," said Benito, "every day islets of verdure, torn from the banks, go drifting down the river. Do they not pass along with their trees, bushes, thickets, rocks, and fields, to lose themselves in the Atlantic 800 leagues away? Why, then, should we not transform our raft into a floating garden?"

"Would you like a forest, miss?" said Fragoso, who stopped at nothing.

"Yes, a forest!" cried the young mulatto; "a forest with its birds and its monkeys—"

"Its snakes, its jaguars!" continued Benito.

"Its Indians, its nomadic tribes," added Manoel, "and even its cannibals!"

"But where are you going to, Fragoso?" said Minha, seeing the active barber making a rush at the bank.

"To look after the forest!" replied Fragoso.

"Useless, my friend," answered the smiling Minha. "Manoel has given me a nosegay and I am quite content. It is true," she added, pointing to the house hidden beneath the flowers, "that he has hidden our house in his betrothal bouquet!"

" To look after the forest !"

CHAPTER IX.

THE EVENING OF THE FIFTH OF JUNE.

WHILE the master's house was being constructed, Joam Garral was also busied in the arrangement of the out-buildings, comprising the kitchen, and offices in which provisions of all kinds were intended to be stored.

In the first place, there was an important stock of the roots of that little tree, some six or ten feet in height, which yields the manioc, and which form the principal food of the inhabitants of these intertropical countries. The root, very much like a long black radish, grows in clumps like potatoes. If it is not poisonous in Africa, it is certain that in South America it contains a more noxious juice, which it is necessary to previously get rid of by pressure. When this result is obtained, the root is reduced to flour, and is then used in many ways, even in the form of tapioca, according to the fancy of the natives.

On board the jangada there was a huge pile of this useful product destined for general consumption.

As for preserved meats, not forgetting a whole flock of sheep, kept in a special stable built in the front, they consisted principally of a quantity of the "presunto" hams of the district, which are of first-class quality; but the guns of the young fellows and of some of the Indians were reckoned on for additional supplies, excellent hunters as they were, to whom there was likely to be no lack of game on the islands and in the forests bordering on the stream. The river was expected to furnish its daily quota; prawns, which ought rather to be called crawfish; "tambagus," the finest fish in the district, of a flavour superior to that of salmon, to which it is often compared; "pirarucus" with red scales, as large as sturgeons, which when salted are used in great quantities throughout Brazil; "candirus," awkward to capture, but good to eat; "piranhas" or devil-fish, striped with red bands, and thirty inches long; turtles large and small, which are counted by millions, and form so large a part of the food of the natives; some of every one of these things it was hoped would figure in turn on the tables of the master and his men.

And so each day shooting and fishing were to be regularly indulged in.

For beverages they had a good store of the best that the country produced; "caysuma" or "machachera," from the Upper and Lower Amazon, an agreeable liquor of slightly acidulated taste, which is distilled from the boiled root of the sweet manioc; "beiju," from Brazil, a sort of national brandy, the "chica" of Peru; the "mazato" of the Ucayali, extracted from the boiled fruits of the banana-tree, pressed and fermented: "guarana," a kind of paste made from the double almond of the "paulliniasorbilis," a genuine tablet of chocolate so far as its colour goes, which is reduced into a fine powder, and with the addition of water yields an excellent drink.

And this was not all. There is in these countries a species of dark violet wine, which is got from the juice of the palm, and the aromatic flavour of this "assais" is greatly appreciated by the Brazilians, and of it there were on board a respectable number of frasques (each holding a little more than half a gallon), which would probably be emptied before they arrived at Para.

The special cellar of the jangada did honour to Benito, who had been appointed its commander-in-chief. Several hundred bottles of sherry, port, and letubal recalled names dear to the earlier conquerors of South America. In addition, the young butler had stored away certain demijohns, holding half a dozen gallons each, of excellent "tafia," a sugared brandy a trifle more pronounced in taste than the national beiju.

As far as tobacco was concerned, there was none of that coarse kind which usually contents the natives of the Amazonian basin. It all came direct from Villa Bella da Imperatriz—or, in other words, from the district in which is grown the best tobacco in Central America.

The principal habitation, with its annexes—kitchen, offices, and cellars—was placed in the rear—or, let us say, stern of the raft—and formed a part reserved for the Garral family and their personal servants.

In the centre the huts for the Indians and the blacks had been erected. The staff were thus placed under the same conditions as at the fazenda of Iquitos, and would always be able to work under the direction of the pilot.

To house the crew a good many huts were required, and these gave to the jangada the appearance of a small village got adrift, and, to tell the truth, it was a better built and better peopled village than many of those on the Upper Amazon.

For the Indians Joam Garral had designed regular cabins—huts without walls, with only light poles supporting the roof of foliage. The air circulated freely throughout these open constructions and swung the hammock suspended in the interior, and the natives, amongst whom were three or four complete families, with women and children, were lodged as if they were on shore.

The blacks here found their customary sheds. They differed from the cabins by being closed in on their four faces, of which one only gave access to the interior. The Indians, accustomed to live in the open air, free and untrammelled, were not able to accustom themselves to the imprisonment of the ajoupas, which agreed better with the life of the blacks.

In the bow regular warehouses had arisen, containing the goods which Joam Garral was carrying to Belem at the same time as the products of his forests.

There, in vast storerooms, under the direction of Benito, the rich cargo had been placed with as much order as if it had carefully been stowed away in a ship's hold.

In the first place, seven thousand arrobas of caoutchouc, each of about thirty pounds, composed the most precious part of the cargo, for every pound of it was worth from three to four francs. The jangada also took fifty hundredweight of sarsaparilla, a smilax which forms an important branch of foreign trade throughout the Amazon districts, and is getting rarer and rarer along the banks of the river, so that the natives are very careful to spare the stems when they gather them. Tonquin beans, known in Brazil under the name of "cumarus," and used in the manufacture of certain essential oils; sassafras, from which is extracted a precious balsam for wounds; bales of dyeing plants, cases of several gums, and a quantity of precious woods, completed a well-adapted cargo for lucrative and easy sale in the provinces of Para.

Some may feel astonished that the number of Indians and negroes embarked were only sufficient to work the raft, and that a larger number were not taken in case of an attack by the riverside Indians.

Such would have been useless. The natives of Central America are not to be feared in the least, and the times are quite changed since it was necessary to provide against their aggressions. The Indians along the river belong to peaceable tribes, and the fiercest of them have retired before the advancing civilization, and drawn farther and farther away from the river and its tributaries. Negro deserters, escaped from the penal colonies of Brazil, England, Holland, or France, are alone to be feared. But there are only a small number of these fugitives, they only move in isolated groups across the savannahs or the woods, and the jangada was, in a measure, secured from any attack on the parts of the backwoodsmen.

On the other hand, there were a number of settlements on the river—towns, villages, and missions. The immense stream no longer traverses a desert, but a basin, which is being colonized day by day. Danger was not taken into consideration. There were no precautions against attacks.

To conclude our description of the jangada, we have only to speak of one or two erections of different kinds, which gave it a very picturesque aspect.

In the bow was the cabin of the pilot—we say in the

bow, and not at the stern, where the helmsman is generally found. In navigating under such circumstances a rudder is of no use. Long oars have no effect on a raft of such dimensions, even when worked with a hundred sturdy arms. It was from the sides, by means of long boat-hooks or props thrust against the bed of the stream, that the jangada was kept in the current, and had its direction altered when going astray. By this means they could range alongside either bank, if they wished for any reason to come to a halt. Three or four ubas, and two pirogues, with the necessary rigging, were carried on board, and afforded easy communications with the banks. The pilot had to look after the channels of the river, the deviations of the current, the eddies which it was necessary to avoid, the creeks or bays which afforded favourable anchorage, and to do this he had to be in the bow.

If the pilot was the material director of this immense machine—for can we not justly call it so?—another personage was its spiritual director; this was Padre Passanha, who had charge of the mission at Iquitos.

A religious family, like that of Joam Garrel's, had availed themselves enthusiastically of this occasion of taking him with them.

Padre Passanha, then aged seventy, was a man of great worth, full of evangelical fervour, charitable and good, and in countries where the representatives of religion are not always examples of the virtues, he stood out as the accomplished type of those great missionaries who have done so much for civilization in the interior of the most savage regions of the world.

For fifty years Padre Passanah had lived at Iquitos, in the mission of which he was the chief. He was loved by all, and worthily so. The Garral family held him in great esteem; it was he who had married the daughter of Farmer Magalhaês to the clerk who had been received at the fazenda. He had known the children from birth; he had baptized them, educated them, and hoped to give each of them the nuptial blessing.

The age of the padre did not allow of his exercising his important ministry any longer. The horn of retreat for him had sounded; he was about to be replaced at Iquitos by a younger missionary, and he was preparing to return into Para, to end his days in one of those convents which are reserved for the old servants of God.

What better occasion could offer than that of descending the river with the family which was as his own? They had proposed it to him, and he had accepted, and when arrived at Belem he was to marry the young couple, Minha and Manoel.

But if Padre Passanha during the course of the voyage was to take his meals with the family, Joam Garral desired to build for him a dwelling apart, and heaven knows what

Araujo the pilot.

Page 111.

care Yaquita and her daughter took to make him comfortable! Assuredly the good old priest had never been so lodged in his modest parsonage!

The parsonage was not enough for Padre Passanha, he ought to have a chapel!

The chapel then was built in the centre of the jangada, and a little bell surmounted it.

It was small enough, undoubtedly, and it could not hold the whole of the crew, but it was richly decorated, and if Joam Garral found his own house on the raft, Padre Passanha had no cause to regret the poverty-stricken church of Iquitos.

Such was the wonderful structure which was going down the Amazon.   It was then on the bank waiting till the flood came to carry it away.   From the observation and calculation of the rising it would seem as though there was not much longer to wait.

All was ready to date, the 5th of June.

The pilot arrived the evening before.   He was a man about fifty, well up in his profession, but rather fond of drink.   Such as he was, Joam Garral in large matters at different times had employed him to take his rafts to Belem, and he had never had cause to repent it.

It is as well to add that Araujo—that was his name—never saw better than when he had imbibed a few glasses of tafia; and he never did any work at all without a cer-

tain demijohn of that liquor to which he paid frequent
· court.

The rise of the flood had clearly manifested itself for
several days. From minute to minute the level of the
river rose, and during the twenty-four hours which preceded the maximum the waters covered the bank on which
the raft rested, but did not lift the raft.

As soon as the movement was assured and there could
be no error as to the height to which the flood would rise,
all those interested in the undertaking were seized with no
little excitement. For if through some inexplicable cause
the waters of the Amazon did not rise sufficiently to flood
the jangada, it would all have to be built over again.
But as the fall of the river would be very rapid it would
take long months before similar conditions recurred.

On the 5th of June, towards the evening, the future
passengers of the jangada were collected on a plateau
which was about a 100 feet above the bank, and waited for
the hour with an anxiety quite intelligible.

There were Yaquita, her daughter, Manoel Valdez,
Padre Passanha, Benito, Lina, Fragoso, Cybele, and some
of the servants, Indian or negro, of the fazenda.

Fragoso could not keep himself still; he went and he
came, he ran down the bank and ran up the plateau, he
noted the points of the river gauge, and shouted " Hurrah!"
as the water crept up.

" It will swim, it will swim!" he shouted. " The raft which is to take us to Belem! It will float if all the cataracts of the sky have to open to flood the Amazon!"

Joam Garral was on the raft with the pilot and some of the crew. It was for him to take all the necessary measures at the critical moment. The jangada was moored to the bank with solid cables, so that it could not be carried away by the current when it floated off.

Quite a tribe of from 150 to 200 Indians, without counting the population of the village, had come to assist at the interesting spectacle.

They were all keenly on the watch, and silence reigned over the impressionable crowd.

Towards five o'clock in the evening the water had reached a level higher than that of the night before—by more than a foot—and the bank had already entirely disappeared beneath the liquid covering.

A certain groaning arose amongst the planks of the enormous structure, but there was still wanting a few inches before it was quite lifted and detached from the ground.

For an hour the groanings increased. The joists grated on all sides. A struggle was going on in which little by little the trunks were being dragged from their sandy bed.

Towards half-past six cries of joy arose. The jangada floated at last, and the current took it towards the middle

I

of the river, but, in obedience to the cables, it quietly took up its position near the bank at the moment that Padre Passanha gave it his blessing, as if it were a vessel launched into the sea whose destinies are in the hands of the Most High!

The start of the Jangada.

Page 115.

CHAPTER X.

FROM IQUITOS TO PEVAS.

ON the 6th of June, the very next day, Joam Garral and his people bade good-bye to the superintendent and the Indians and negroes who were to stay behind at the fazenda. At six o'clock in the morning the jangada received all its passengers, or rather inhabitants, and each of them took possession of his cabin, or perhaps we had better say his house.

The moment of departure had come. Araujo, the pilot, got into his place at the bow, and the crew, armed with their long poles, went to their proper quarters.

Joam Garral, assisted by Benito and Manoel, superintended the unmooring.

At the command of the pilot the ropes were eased off, and the poles applied to the bank so as to give the jangada a start. The current was not long in seizing it, and coasting the left bank, the islands of Iquitos and Parianta were passed to the right.

The voyage had commenced—where would it finish ?   In Para, at Belem, eight hundred leagues from this little Peruvian village, if nothing happened to modify the route. How would it finish ?   That was the secret of the future.

The weather was magnificent. A pleasant " pampero " tempered the ardour of the sun—one of those winds which in June or July come from off the Cordilleras, many hundred leagues away, after having swept across the huge plain of the Sacramento.   Had the raft been provided with masts and sails she would have felt the effects of the breeze, and her speed would have been greater; but owing to the sinuosities of the river and its abrupt changes, which they were bound to follow, they had had to renounce such assistance.

In a flat district like that through which the Amazon flows, which is almost a boundless plain, the gradient of the river-bed is scarcely perceptible.   It has been calculated that between Tabatinga on the Brazilian frontier, and the source of this huge body of water, the difference of level does not exceed a decimetre in each league.   There is no other river in the world whose inclination is so slight.

It follows from this that the average speed of the current cannot be estimated at more than two leagues in the twenty-four hours, and sometimes, while the droughts are on, it is even less. However, during the period of the floods it has been known to increase to between thirty and forty kilometres.

Happily, it was under these latter conditions that the jangada was to proceed ; but, cumbrous in its movements, it could not keep up to the speed of the current which ran past it. There are also to be taken into account the stoppages occasioned by the bends of the river, the numerous islands which had to be rounded, the shoals which had to be avoided, and the hours of halting, which were necessarily lost when the night was too dark to advance securely, so that we cannot allow more than twenty-five kilometres for each twenty-four hours.

In addition, the surface of the water is far from being completely clear. Trees still green, vegetable remains, islets of plants constantly torn from the banks, formed quite a flotilla of fragments carried on by the currents, and were so many obstacles to speedy navigation.

The mouth of the Nanay was soon passed, and lost to sight behind a point on the left bank, which, with its carpet of russet grasses tinted by the sun, formed a ruddy relief to the green forests on the horizon.

The jangada took the centre of the stream between the numerous picturesque islands, of which there are a dozen between Iquitos and Pulcalppa.

Araujo, who did not forget to clear his vision and his memory by an occasional application to his demijohn, manœuvred very ably when passing through this archipelago. At his word of command fifty poles from each side of the raft were raised in the air, and struck the water with an automatic movement very curious to behold.

While this was going on, Yaquita, aided by Lina and Cybele, was getting everything in order, and the Indian cooks were preparing the breakfast.

As for the two young fellows and Minha, they were walking up and down in company with Padre Passanha, and from time to time the lady stopped and watered the plants which were placed about the base of the dwelling-house.

"Well, padre," said Benito, "do you know a more agreeable way of travelling?"

"No, my dear boy," replied the padre; "it is truly travelling with all one's belongings!"

"And without any fatigue!" added Manoel; "we might do hundreds of thousands of miles in this way!"

"And," said Minha, "you do not repent having taken passage with us? Does it not seem to you as if we were afloat on an island drifted quietly away from the bed of the river with its prairies and its trees? Only—"

"Only?" repeated the padre.

"Only we have made the island with our own hands; it belongs to us, and I prefer it to all the islands of the Amazon! I have a right to be proud of it!"

"Yes, my daughter; and I absolve you from your pride. Besides, I am not allowed to scold you in the presence of Manoel!"

"But, on the other hand," replied she, gaily, "you should teach Manoel to scold me when I deserve it. He is a great deal too indulgent to my little self."

"Well, then, dear Minha," said Manoel, "I shall profit by that permission to remind you—"

"Of what?"

"That you were very busy in the library at the fazenda, and that you promised to make me very learned about everything connected with the Upper Amazon. We know very little about it in Para, and here we have been passing several islands and you have not even told me their names!"

"What is the good of that?" said she.

"Yes; what is the good of it?" repeated Benito. "What can be the use of remembering the hundreds of names in the 'Tupi' dialect with which these islands are dressed out? It is enough to know them. The Americans are much more practical with their Mississippi islands; they number them—"

"As they number the avenues and streets of their towns," replied Manoel. "Frankly, I don't care much for that numerical system; it conveys nothing to the imagination—Sixty-fourth Island or Sixty-fifth Island, any more than Sixth Street or Third Avenue. Don't you agree with me, Minha ?"

"Yes, Manoel ; though I am of somewhat the same way of thinking as my brother. But even if we do not know their names, the islands of our great river are truly splendid ! See how they rest under the shadows of those gigantic palm-trees with their drooping leaves ! And the girdle of reeds which encircles them through which a pirogue can with difficulty make its way ! And the mangrove-trees, whose fantastic roots buttress them to the bank like the claws of some gigantic crab ! Yes, the islands are beautiful, but, beautiful as they are, they cannot equal the one we have made our own !"

"My little Minha is enthusiastic to-day," said the padre.

"Ah, padre ! I am so happy to see everybody happy around me !"

At this moment the voice of Yaquita was heard calling Minha into the house.

The young girl smilingly ran off.

"You will have an amiable companion," said the padre. "All the joy of the house goes away with you, my friend."

"Brave little sister !" said Benito, "we shall miss her greatly, and the padre is right. However, if you do not marry her, Manoel—there is still time—she will stay with us."

"She will stay with you, Benito," replied Manoel. "Believe me, I have a presentiment that we shall all be
reunited!"

The first day passed capitally; breakfast, dinner, siesta,
walks, all took place as if Joam Garral and his people were
still in the comfortable fazenda of Iquitos.

During these twenty-four hours the mouths of the rivers
Bacali, Chochio, Pucalppa, on the left of the stream, and
those of the rivers Itinicari, Maniti, Moyoc, Tucuya, and
the islands of this name on the right, were passed without
accident. The night, lighted by the moon, allowed them
to save a halt, and the giant raft glided peacefully on along
the surface of the Amazon.

On the morrow, the 7th of June, the jangada breasted
the banks of the village of Pucalppa, named also New
Oran. Old Oran, situated fifteen leagues down stream on
the same left bank of the river, is almost abandoned for
the new settlement, whose population consists of Indians
belonging to the Mayoruna and Orejone tribes. Nothing
can be more picturesque than this village with its ruddy-
coloured banks, its unfinished church, its cottages, whose
chimneys are hidden amid the palms, and its two or three
ubas half stranded on the shore.

During the whole of the 7th of June the jangada continued to follow the left bank of the river, passing several
unknown tributaries of no importance. For a moment

there was a chance of her grounding on the easterly shore of the island of Sinicuro ; but the pilot, well served by the crew, warded off the danger and remained in the flow of the stream.

In the evening they arrived alongside a narrow island, called Napo Island, from the name of the river which here comes in from the north-north-west, and mingles its waters with those of the Amazon through a mouth about 800 yards across, after having watered the territories of the Coto and Orejone Indians.

It was on the morning of the 7th of June that the jangada was abreast the little island of Mango, which causes the Napo to split into two streams before falling into the Amazon.

Several years later a French traveller, Paul Marcoy, went out to examine the colour of the waters of this tributary, which has been graphically compared to the cloudy greenish opal of absinthe. At the same time he corrected some of the measurements of La Condamine. But then the mouth of the Napo was sensibly increased by the floods, and it was with a good deal of rapidity that its current, coming from the eastern slopes of Cotopaxi, hurried fiercely to mingle itself with the tawny waters of the Amazon.

A few Indians had wandered to the mouth of this river. They were robust in build, of tall stature, with shaggy hair,

The Indians on the river bank. .

Page 122.

and had their noses pierced with a rod of palm, and the lobes of their ears lengthened to their shoulders by the weight of heavy rings of precious wood. Some women were with them. None of them showed any intention of coming on board. It is asserted that these natives are cannibals ; but if that is true—and it is said of many of the riverine tribes—there must have been more evidence for the cannibalism than we get to-day.

Some hours later the village of Bella Vista, situated on a somewhat lower bank, appeared, with its cluster of magnificent trees, towering above a few huts roofed with straw, over which there drooped the large leaves of some medium-sized banana-trees, like waters overflowing from a tazza.

Then the pilot, so as to follow a better current, which turned off from the bank, directed the raft towards the right side of the river, which he had not yet approached. The manœuvre was not accomplished without certain difficulties, which were successfully overcome after a good many resorts to the demijohn.

This allowed them to notice in passing some of those numerous lagoons with black waters, which are distributed along the course of the Amazon, and which often have no communication with the river. One of these, bearing the name of the Lagoon of Oran, is of fair size, and receives the water by a large strait. In the middle of the stream are scattered several islands and two or three islets curiously grouped; and on the opposite bank Benito recognized the site of the ancient Oran, of which they could only see a few uncertain traces.

During two days the jangada travelled sometimes under the left bank, sometimes under the right, according to the condition of the current, without giving the least sign of grounding.

The passengers had already become used to this new life. Joam Garral leaving to his son everything that referred to the commercial side of the expedition, kept himself principally to his room, thinking and writing. What he was writing about he told to nobody, not even Yaquita, and it seemed to have already assumed the importance of a veritable essay.

Benito, all observation, chatted with the pilot and acted as manager. Yaquita, her daughter, and Manoel, nearly always formed a group apart, discussing their future projects just as they had walked and done in the park of the fazenda. The life was, in fact, the same. Not quite, perhaps, to Benito, who had not yet found occasion to participate in the pleasures of the chase. If, however, the forests of Iquitos failed him with their wild beasts, agoutis, peccaries, and cabiais, the birds flew in flocks from the banks of the river and fearlessly perched on the jangada. When they were of such quality as to figure fairly on the

The Jangada moored for the night.

Page 125.

table, Benito shot them; and, in the interest of all, his sister raised no objection; but if he came across any grey or yellow herons, or red or white ibises, which haunt the sides, he spared them through love for Minha. One single species of grebe, which is uneatable, found no grace in the eyes of the young merchant: this was the " caiarara," as quick to dive as to swim or fly; a bird with a disagreeable cry, but whose down bears a high price in the different markets of the Amazonian basin.

At length, after having passed the village of Omaguas and the mouth of the Ambiacu, the jangada arrived at Pevas on the evening of the 11th of June, and was moored to the bank.

As it was to remain here for some hours before nightfall, Benito disembarked, taking with him the ever-ready Fragoso, and the two sportsmen started off to beat the thickets in the environs of the little place. An agouti and a cabiai, not to mention a dozen partridges, enriched the larder after this fortunate excursion. At Pevas, where there is a population of 260 inhabitants, Benito would perhaps have done some trade with the lay brothers of the mission, who are at the same time wholesale merchants, but these had just sent away some bales of sarsaparilla and arrobas of caoutchouc towards the Lower Amazon, and their stores were empty.

The jangada departed at daybreak, and passed the little archipelago of the Iatio and Cochiquinas islands, after having left the village of the latter name on the right. Several mouths of smaller unnamed affluents showed themselves on the right of the river through the spaces between the islands.

Many natives, with shaved heads, tattooed cheeks and foreheads, carrying plates of metal in the lobes of their ears, noses, and lower lips, appeared for an instant on the shore. They were armed with arrows and blow-tubes, but made no use of them, and did not even attempt to communicate with the jangada.

The Indians on the island.

Page 126.

Fishing.

Page 127.

CHAPTER XI.

FROM PEVAS TO THE FRONTIER.

DURING the few days which followed nothing occurred worthy of note. The nights were so fine that the long raft went on its way with the stream without even a halt. The two picturesque banks of the river seemed to change like the panoramas of the theatres which unroll from one wing to another. By a kind of optical illusion it appeared as though the raft was motionless between two moving pathways.

Benito had no shooting on the banks, for no halt was made, but game was very advantageously replaced by the results of the fishing.

A great variety of excellent fish were taken—"pacos," "surubis," "gamitanas," of exquisite flavour, and several of those large rays called "duridaris," with rose-coloured stomachs and black backs armed with highly poisonous darts. There were also collected by thousands those "candirus," a kind of small silurus, of which many are microscopic, and which so frequently make a pincushion of the calves of the bather when he imprudently ventures into their haunts.

The rich waters of the Amazon were also frequented by many other aquatic animals, which escorted the jangada through its waves for whole hours together.

There were the gigantic " pira-rucus," ten and twelve feet long, cuirassed with large scales with scarlet borders, whose flesh was not much appreciated by the natives. Neither did they care to capture many of the graceful dolphins which played about in hundreds, striking with their tails the planks of the raft, gambolling at the bow and stern, and making the water alive with coloured reflections and spurts of spray, which the refracted light converted into so many rainbows.

On the 16th of June the jangada, after fortunately clearing several shallows in approaching the banks, arrived near the large island of San Pablo, and the following evening she stopped at the village of Moromoros, which is situated on the left side of the Amazon. Twenty-four hours afterwards, passing the mouths of the Atacoari or Cocha—or rather the "furo," or canal, which communicates with the lake of Cabello-Cocha on the right bank—she put in at the rising ground of the Mission of Cocha. This was the country of the Marahua Indians, whose long floating hair, and mouths opening in the middle of a kind of fan made of the spines of palm-trees, six inches long, give them a cat-like look—their endeavour being, according to Paul Marcoy, to resemble the tiger, whose boldness, strength, and cunning they admire above everything. Several women came with these Marahuas, smoking cigars, but holding the lighted ends in their teeth. All of them, like the king of the Amazonian forests, go about almost naked.

The mission of Cocha was then in charge of a Franciscan monk, who was anxious to visit Padre Passanha.

Joam Garral received him with a warm welcome, and offered him a seat at the dinner-table.

On that day was given a dinner which did honour to the Indian cook. The traditional soup of fragrant herbs; cake, so often made to replace bread in Brazil, composed of the flour of the manioc thoroughly impregnated with the gravy of meat and tomato jelly; poultry with rice, swimming in a sharp sauce made of vinegar and "malagueta;" a dish of spiced herbs, and cold cake sprinkled with cinnamon, formed enough to tempt a poor monk reduced to the ordinary meagre fare of his parish. They tried all they could to detain him, and Yaquita and her daughter did their utmost in persuasion. But the Franciscan had to visit on that evening an Indian who was lying ill at Cocha, and he heartily thanked the hospitable family, and departed, not without taking a few presents,

K

which would be well received by the neophytes of the mission.

For two days Araujo was very busy. The bed of the river gradually enlarged, but the islands became more numerous, and the current, embarrassed by these obstacles, increased in strength. Great care was necessary in passing between the islands of Cabello-Cocha, Tarapote, and Cacao. Many stoppages had to be made, and occasionally they were obliged to pole off the jangada, which now and then threatened to run aground. Every one assisted in the work, and it was under these difficult circumstances that, on the eveniug of the 20th of June, they found themselves at Nuestra-Senora-di-Loreto.

Loreto is the last Peruvian town situated on the left bank of the river before arriving at the Brazilian frontier. It is only a little village, composed of about twenty houses, grouped on a slightly undulating bank, formed of ochreous earth and clay.

It was in 1770 that this mission was founded by the Jesuit missionaries. The Ticuma Indians, who inhabit the territories on the north of the river, are natives with ruddy skins, bushy hair, and striped designs on their faces, making them look like the lacquer on a Chinese table. Both men and women are simply clothed, with cotton bands bound round their thighs and stomachs. They are now not more than two hundred in number; and on the banks of the

Atacoari are found the last traces of a nation which was formerly so powerful under its famous chiefs.

At Loreto there also live a few Peruvian soldiers and two or three Portuguese merchants, trading in cotton stuffs, salt fish, and sarsaparilla.

Benito went ashore, to buy, if possible, a few bales of this smilax, which is always so much in demand in the markets of the Amazon. Joam Garral, occupied all the time in the work which gave him not a moment's rest, did not stir. Yaquita, her daughter, and Manoel also remained on board. The mosquitoes of Loreto have a deserved reputation for driving away such visitors as do not care to leave much of their blood with the redoubtable diptera.

Manoel had a few appropriate words to say about these insects, and they were not of a nature to encourage an inclination to brave their stings.

" They say that all the new species which infest the banks of the Amazon collect at the village of Loreto. I believe it, but do not wish to confirm it. There, Minha, you can take your choice between the grey mosquito, the hairy mosquito, the white-clawed mosquito, the dwarf mosquito, the trumpeter, the little fifer, the urtiquis, the harlequin, the big black, and the red of the woods ; or rather they may take their choice of you for a little repast, and you will come back hardly recognizable ! I fancy these bloodthirsty diptera guard the Brazilian frontier considerably better than the poverty-stricken soldiers we see on the bank."

"But if everything is of use in nature," asked Minha, "what is the use of mosquitoes?"

"They minister to the happiness of entomologists," replied Manoel; "and I should be much embarrassed to find a better explanation."

What Manoel had said of the Loreto mosquitoes was only too true. When Benito had finished his business and returned on board, his face and hands were tattoed with thousands of red points, without counting some chigoes, which, in spite of the leather of his boots, had introduced themselves beneath his toes.

"Let us set off this very instant," said Benito, "or these wretched insects will invade us, and the jangada will become uninhabitable!"

"And we shall take them into Para," said Manoel, "where there are already quite enough for its own needs."

And so, in order not to pass even the night near the banks, the jangada pushed off into the stream.

On leaving Loreto the Amazon turns slightly towards the south-west, between the islands of Arava, Cuyari, and Urucutea. The jangada then glided along the black waters of the Cajaru, as they mingled with the white stream of the Amazon. After having passed this tributary on the left, it peacefully arrived during the evening of the 23rd of June alongside the large island of Jahuma.

The setting of the sun on a clear horizon, free from all haze, announced one of those beautiful tropical nights which are unknown in the temperate zones. A light breeze freshened the air ; the moon arose in the constellated depths of the sky, and for several hours took the place of the twilight which is absent from these latitudes. But even during this period the stars shone with unequalled purity. The immense plain seemed to stretch into the infinite like a sea, and at the extremity of the axis, which measures more than two hundred thousand millions of leagues, there appeared on the north the single diamond of the pole star, on the south the four brilliants of the Southern Cross.

The trees on the left bank and on the island of Jahuma stood up in sharp black outline. There were recognizable in the undecided *silhouettes* the trunks, or rather columns, of "copahus," which spread out in umbrellas, groups of "sandis," from which is extracted the thick and sugared milk, intoxicating as wine itself, and "vignaticos" eighty feet high, whose summits shake at the passage of the lightest currents of air. "What a magnificent sermon are these forests of the Amazon!" has been justly said. Yes ; and we might add, "What a magnificent hymn there is in the nights of the tropics!"

The birds were giving forth their last evening notes—
"bentivis," who hang their nests on the bankside reeds;
"niambus," a kind of partridge, whose song is composed
of four notes, in perfect accord; "kamichis," with their
plaintive melody; kingfishers, whose call responds like a
signal to the last cry of their congeners; "canindes," with
their sonorous trumpets; and red macaws, who fold their
wings in the foliage of the "jaquetibas," when night comes
on to dim their glowing colours.

On the jangada every one was at his post, in the
attitude of repose. The pilot alone, standing in the bow,
showed his tall stature, scarcely defined in the earlier
shadows. The watch, with his long pole on his shoulder,
reminded one of an encampment of Tartar horsemen. The
Brazilian flag hung from the top of the staff in the bow,
and the breeze was scarcely strong enough to lift the
bunting.

At eight o'clock the three first tinklings of the Angelus
escaped from the bell of the little chapel. The three
tinklings of the second and third verses sounded in their
turn, and the salutation was completed in the series of
more rapid strokes of the little bell.

However, the family after this July day remained
sitting under the verandah to breathe the fresh air from
the open.

It had been so each evening, and while Joam Garral,

The crew at quarters.

Page 134.

always silent, was contented to listen, the young people gaily chatted away till bedtime.

"Ah! our splendid river! our magnificent Amazon!" exclaimed the young girl, whose enthusiasm for the immense stream never failed.

"Unequalled river, in very truth!" said Manoel; "and I do not understand all its sublime beauties! We are going down it, however, like Orellana and La Condamine did so many centuries ago, and I am not at all surprised at their marvellous descriptions."

"A little fabulous," replied Benito.

"Now, brother," said Minha seriously, "say no evil of our Amazon."

"To remind you that it has its legends, my sister, is to say no ill of it."

"Yes, that is true; and it has some marvellous ones!" replied Minha.

"What legends?" asked Manoel. "I dare avow that they have not yet found their way into Para—or rather that, for my part, I am not acquainted with them."

"What, then, do you learn in the Belem colleges?" laughingly asked Minha.

"I begin to perceive that they teach us nothing," replied Manoel.

"What, sir!" replied Minha, with a pleasant seriousness, "you do not know, among other fables, that an enormous reptile called the 'minhocao' sometimes visits the Amazon, and that the waters of the river rise or fall according as this serpent plunges in or quits them, so gigantic is he!"

"But have you ever seen this phenomenal minhocao?"

"Alas, no!" replied Lina.

"What a pity!" Fragoso thought it proper to add.

"And the 'Mae d'Aqua,'" continued the girl—"that proud and redoubtable woman whose look fascinates and drags beneath the waters of the river the imprudent ones who gaze at her!"

"Oh, as for the 'Mae d'Aqua,' she exists!" cried the naive Lina; "they say that she still walks on the banks, but disappears like a water-sprite as soon as you approach her."

"Very well, Lina," said Benito; "the first time you see her, just let me know."

"So that she may seize you and take you to the bottom of the river? Never, Mr. Benito!"

"She believes it!" shouted Minha.

"There are people who believe in the trunk of Manaos!" said Fragoso, always ready to intervene on behalf of Lina.

"The 'trunk of Manaos'?" asked Manoel. "What about the trunk of Manaos?"

"Mr. Manoel," answered Fragoso, with comic gravity,

"it appears that there is—or rather formerly was—a trunk of 'turuma,' which every year at the same time descended the Rio Negro, stopping several days at Manaos, and going on into Para, halting at every port, where the natives ornamented it with little flags. Arrived at Belem, it came to a halt, turned back on its road, remounted the Amazon to the Rio Negro, and returned to the forest from which it had mysteriously started. One day somebody tried to drag it ashore, but the river rose in anger, and the attempt had to be given up. And on another occasion the captain of a ship harpooned it and tried to tow it along. This time again the river, in anger, broke off the ropes, and the trunk mysteriously escaped."

"What became of it?" asked the mulatto.

"It appears that on its last voyage, Miss Lina," replied Fragoso, "it mistook the way, and instead of going up the Negro it continued in the Amazon, and it has never been seen again."

"Oh, if we could only meet it!" said Lina.

"If we meet it," answered Benito, "we will put you on it! It will take you back to the mysterious forest, and you will likewise pass into the state of a legendary naiad!"

"And why not?" asked the mulatto.

"So much for your legends," said Manoel; "and I think your river is worthy of them. But it has also its histories, which are worth something more. I know one, and if I

were not afraid of grieving you—for it is a very sad one—
I would relate it."

"Oh! tell it, by all means, Mr. Manoel," exclaimed
Lina; "I like stories which make you cry!"

"What, do you cry, Lina?" said Benito.

"Yes, Mr. Benito; but I cry when laughing."

"Oh, well! let us have it, Manoel!"

"It is the history of a Frenchwoman whose sorrows
rendered these banks memorable in the eighteenth century."

"We are listening," said Minha.

"Here goes, then," said Manoel. "In 1741, at the time
of the expedition of the two Frenchmen, Bouguer and
La Condamine, who were sent to measure a terrestrial
degree on the Equator, they were accompanied by a very
distinguished astronomer, Godin des Odonais. Godin des
Odonais set out then, but he did not set out alone, for the
New World; he took with him his young wife, his
children, his father-in-law, and his brother-in-law. The
travellers arrived at Quito in good health. There there
commenced a series of misfortunes for Madame Odonais;
in a few months she lost some of her children. When
Godin des Odonais had completed his work, towards the
end of the year 1759, he left Quito and started for
Cayenne. Once arrived in this town he wanted his family
to come to him, but war had been declared, and he was

obliged to ask the Portuguese Government for permission for a free passage for Madame Odonais and her people. What do you think? Many years passed before the permission could be given. In 1765 Godin des Odonais, maddened by the delay, resolved to ascend the Amazon in search of his wife at Quito; but at the moment of his departure a sudden illness stopped him, and he could not carry out his intention. However, his application had not been useless, and Madame des Odonais learnt at last that the King of Portugal had given the necessary permission, and prepared to embark and descend the river to her husband. At the same time an escort was ordered to be ready in the missions of the Upper Amazon. Madame des Odonais was a woman of great courage, as you will see presently; she never hesitated, and notwithstanding the dangers of such a voyage across the Continent, she started."

"It was her duty to her husband, Manoel," said Yaquita, "and I would have done the same."

"Madame des Odonais," continued Manoel, "came to Rio Bamba, at the south of Quito, bringing her brother-in-law, her children, and a French doctor. Their endeavour was to reach the missions on the Brazilian frontier, where they hoped to find a ship and the escort. The voyage at first was favourable; it was made down the tributaries of the Amazon in a canoe. The difficulties, however gradually increased with the dangers and fatigues in a country decimated by the small-pox. Of several guides who offered their services, the most part disappeared after a few days; one of them, the last who remained faithful to the travellers, was drowned in the Bobonasa, in endeavouring to help the French doctor. At length the canoe, damaged by rocks and floating trees, became useless. It was therefore necessary to get on shore, and there at the edge of the impenetrable forest they built a few huts of foliage. The doctor offered to go on in front with a negro who had never wished to leave Madame des Odonais. The two went off; they waited for them several days, but in vain. They never returned.

"In the meantime the victuals were getting exhausted. The forsaken ones in vain endeavoured to descend the Bobonasa on a raft. They had to again take to the forest, and make their way on foot through the almost impenetrable undergrowth. The fatigues were too much for the poor folks! They died off one by one in spite of the cares. of the noble Frenchwoman. At the end of a few days children, relations, and servants, all were dead!"

"What an unfortunate woman!" said Lina.

"Madame des Odonais alone remained," continued Manoel. "There she was, at a thousand leagues from the ocean which she was trying to reach! It was no longer a mother who continued her journey towards the river—

Passing the frontier.

Page 141.

the mother had lost her children; she had buried them with her own hands! It was a wife who wished to see her husband once again! She travelled night and day, and at length regained the Bobonasa. She was there received by some kind-hearted Indians, who took her to the missions, where the escort was waiting. But she arrived alone, and behind her the stages of the route were marked with graves! Madame des Odonais reached Loreto, where we were a few days back. From this Peruvian village she descended the Amazon, as we are doing at this moment, and at length she rejoined her husband after a separation of nineteen years."

"Poor lady!" said Minha.

"Above all, poor mother!" answered Yaquita.

At this moment Araujo, the pilot, came aft and said,—

"Joam Garral, we are off the Ronde Island. We are passing the frontier!"

"The frontier!" replied Joam.

And rising, he went to the side of the jangada, and looked long and earnestly at the Ronde Island, with the waves breaking up against it. Then his hand sought his forehead, as if to rid himself of some remembrance.

"The frontier!" murmured he, bowing his head by an involuntary movement.

But an instant after his head was raised, and his expression was that of a man resolved to do his duty to the last.

CHAPTER XII.

FRAGOSO AT WORK.

"BRAZA" (burning embers) is a word found in the Spanish language as far back as the twelfth century. It has been used to make the word "brazil," as descriptive of certain woods which yield a reddish dye. From this has come the name "Brazil," given to that vast district of South America which is crossed by the equator, and in which these products are so frequently met with. In very early days these woods were the object of considerable trade. Although correctly called "ibirapitunga," from the place of production, the name of "brazil" stuck to them, and it has become that of the country, which seems like an immense heap of embers lighted by the rays of the tropical sun.

Brazil was from the first occupied by the Portuguese. About the commencement of the sixteenth century, Alvarez Cabral, the pilot, took possession of it, and although France and Holland partially established themselves there, it has remained Portuguese, and possesses all the qualities which distinguish that gallant little nation.

It is to-day one of the largest states of Central America, and has at its head the intelligent artist-king Don Pedro.

"What is your privilege in the tribe?" asked Montaigne, of an Indian whom he met at Havre.

"The privilege of marching first to battle!" innocently answered the Indian.

War, we know, was for a long time the surest and most rapid vehicle of civilization. The Brazilians did what this Indian did: they fought, they defended their conquests they enlarged them, and we see them marching in the first rank of the civilizing advance.

It was in 1824, sixteen years after the foundation of the Portugo-Brazilian Empire, that Brazil proclaimed its independence by the voice of Don Juan, whom the French armies had chased from Portugal.

It remained only to define the frontier between the new empire and that of its neighbour, Peru. This was no easy matter.

If Brazil wished to extend to the Rio Napo in the west, Peru attempted to reach eight degrees farther, as far as the Lake of Ega.

But in the meantime Brazil had to interfere to hinder the kidnapping of the Indians from the Amazon, a practice which was engaged in much to the profit of the Hispano-Brazilian Missions. There was no better method

of checking this trade than that of fortifying the Island of
the Ronde, a little above Tabatinga, and there establishing
a post.

This afforded the solution, and from that time the
frontier of the two countries passed through the middle of
this island.

Above, the river is Peruvian, and is called the Marañon,
as has been said. Below, it is Brazilian, and takes the
name of the Amazon.

It was on the evening of the 25th of June that the jangada
'stopped before Tabatinga, the first Brazilian town situated
on the left bank at the entrance of the river of which it
bears the name, and belonging to the parish of St. Paul,
established on the right a little farther down stream.

Joam Garral had decided to pass six-and-thirty hours
here, so as to give a little rest to the crew. They would
not start, therefore, until the morning of the 27th.

On this occasion Yaquita and her children, less likely,
perhaps, than at Iquitos to be fed upon by the native
mosquitoes, had announced their intention of going on shore
and visiting the town.

The population of Tabatinga is estimated at four
hundred, nearly all Indians, comprising, no doubt, many of
those wandering families who are never settled at particular
spots on the banks of the Amazon or its smaller tributaries.

Tabatinga.

Page 144.

The post at the Island of the Ronde has been abandoned for some years, and transferred to Tabatinga. It can thus be called a garrison town, but the garrison is only composed of nine soldiers, nearly all Indians, and a sergeant, who is the actual commandant of the place.

A bank about thirty feet high, in which are cut the steps of a not very solid staircase, forms here the curtain of the esplanade which carries the pigmy fort. The house of the commandant consists of a couple of huts placed in a square, and the soldiers occupy an oblong building a hundred feet away, at the foot of a large tree.

The collection of cabins exactly resembles all the villages and hamlets which are scattered along the banks of the river, although in them a flagstaff carrying the Brazilian colours does not rise above a sentry-box, for ever destitute of its sentinel, nor are four small mortars present to cannonade on an emergency any vessel which does not come in when ordered.

As for the village properly so called, it is situated below, at the base of the plateau. A road, which is but a ravine shaded by ficuses and miritis, leads to it in a few minutes. There, on a half-cracked hill of clay, stand a dozen houses, covered with the leaves of the "boiassu" palm placed round a central space.

All this is not very curious, but the environs of Tabatinga are charming, particularly at the mouth of the Javary,

L

which is of sufficient extent to contain the Archipelago of the Aramasa Islands. Hereabouts are grouped many fine trees, and amongst them a large number of the palms, whose supple fibres are used in the fabrication of hammocks and fishing-nets, and are the cause of some trade. To conclude, the place is one of the most picturesque on the Upper Amazon.

Tabatinga is destined to become before long a station of some importance, and will no doubt rapidly develope, for there will stop the Brazilian steamers which ascend the river, and the Peruvian steamers which descend it. There they will tranship passengers and cargoes. It does not require much for an English or American village to become in a few years the centre of considerable commerce.

The river is very beautiful along this part of its course. The influence of ordinary tides is not perceptible at Tabatinga, which is more than six hundred leagues from the Atlantic. But it is not so with the "pororoca," that species of eddy which for three days in the height of the syzygies raises the waters of the Amazon, and turns them back at the rate of seventeen kilometres per hour. They say that the effects of this bore are felt up to the Brazilian frontier.

On the morrow, the 26th of June, the Garral family prepared to go off and visit the village. Though Joam, Benito, and Manoel had already set foot in a Brazilian town, it was otherwise with Yaquita and her daughter ; for them it was, so to speak, a taking possession. It is conceivable, therefore, that Yaquita and Minha should attach some importance to the event.

If, on his part, Fragoso, in his capacity of wandering barber, had already run through the different provinces of Central America, Lina, like her young mistress, had never been on Brazilian soil.

But before leaving the jangada Fragoso had sought Joam Garral, and had the following conversation with him.

"Mr. Garral," said he, "from the day when you received me at the fazenda of Iquitos, lodged, clothed, fed—in a word, took me in so hospitably—I have owed you—"

"You owe me absolutely nothing, my friend," answered Joam, "so do not insist—"

"Oh, do not be alarmed!" exclaimed Fragoso, "I am not going to pay it off! Let me add, that you took me on board the jangada and gave me the means of descending the river. But here we are, on the soil of Brazil, which, according to all probability, I ought never to have seen again. Without that liana—"

"It is to Lina, and to Lina alone, that you should tender your thanks," said Joam.

"I know," said Fragoso, "and I will never forget what I owe her, any more than what I owe you."

"They tell me, Fragoso," continued Joam, "that you are going to say good-bye, and intend to remain at Tabatinga."

"By no means, Mr. Garral, since you have allowed me to accompany you to Belem, where I hope at the least to be able to resume my old trade."

"Well, if that is your intention—what were you going to ask me?"

"I was going to ask if you saw any inconvenience in my working at my profession on our route. There is no necessity for my hand to rust; and, besides, a few handfuls of reis would not be so bad at the bottom of my pocket, more particularly if I had earned them. You know, Mr. Garral, that a barber who is also a hairdresser—and I hardly like to say a doctor, out of respect to Mr. Manoel —always finds customers in these Upper Amazon villages."

"Particularly among the Brazilians," answered Joam. "As for the natives—"

"I beg pardon," replied Fragoso, "particularly among the natives. Ah! although there is no beard to trim—for nature has been very stingy towards them in that way— there are always some heads of hair to be dressed in the latest fashion. They are very fond of it, these savages, both the men and the women! I shall not be installed ten minutes in the square at Tabatinga, with my cup and ball in hand—the cup and ball I have brought on board, and which I can manage with pretty pleasantly—before a circle of braves and squaws will have formed around me. They will struggle for my favours. I could remain here for a month, and the whole tribe of the Ticunas would come to me to have their hair looked after! They won't hesitate to make the acquaintance of "curling tongs"— that is what they will call me—if I revisit the walls of Tabatinga! I have already had two tries here, and my scissors and comb have done marvels! It does not do to return too often on the same track. The Indian ladies don't have their hair curled every day, like the beauties of our Brazilian cities. No; when it is done, it is done for a year, and during the twelvemonth they will take every care not to endanger the edifice which I have raised—with what talent I dare not say. Now it is nearly a year since I was at Tabatinga; I go to find my monuments in ruin! And if it is not objectionable to you, Mr. Garral, I would render myself again worthy of the reputation which I have acquired in these parts, the question of reis, and not that of conceit, being, you understand, the principal."

"Go on, then, friend," replied Joam Garral, laughingly; "but be quick! we can only remain a day at Tabatinga, and we shall start to-morrow at dawn."

"I will not lose a minute," answered Fragoso—"just time to take the tools of my profession, and I am off!"

"Off you go, Fragoso!" said Joam, "and may the reis rain into your pocket!"

"Yes; and that is a proper sort of rain, and there can never be too much of it for your obedient servant."

And so saying, Fragoso rapidly moved away.

A moment afterwards the family, with the exception of Joam, went ashore. The jangada was able to approach near enough to the bank for the landing to take place without trouble. A staircase, in a miserable state, cut in the cliff, allowed the visitors to arrive on the crest of the plateau.

Yaquita and her party were received by the commandant of the fort, a poor fellow who, however, knew the laws of hospitality, and offered them some breakfast in his cottage. Here and there passed and re-passed several soldiers on guard, while on the threshold of the barrack appeared a few children, with their mothers of Ticuna blood, affording very poor specimens of the mixed race.

In place of accepting the breakfast of the sergeant, Yaquita invited the commandant and his wife to come and have theirs on board the jangada.

The commandant did not wait for a second invitation, and an appointment was made for eleven o'clock. In the meantime Yaquita, her daughter, and the young mulatto, accompanied by Manoel, went for a walk in the neighbourhood, leaving Benito to settle with the commandant about the tolls—he being chief of the custom-house as well as of the military establishment.

That done, Benito, as was his wont, strolled off with his gun into the adjoining woods. On this occasion Manoel had declined to accompany him. Fragoso had left the jangada, but instead of mounting to the fort he had made for the village, crossing the ravine which led off from the right on the level of the bank. He reckoned more on the native custom of Tabatinga than on that of the garrison. Doubtless the soldiers' wives would not have wished better than to have been put under his hands, but the husbands scarcely cared to part with a few reis for the sake of gratifying the whims of their coquettish partners.

Among the natives it was quite the reverse. Husbands and wives, the jolly barber knew them well, and he knew they would give him a better reception.

Behold, then, Fragoso on the road, coming up the shady lane beneath the ficuses, and arriving in the central square of Tabatinga!

As soon as he set foot in the place the famous barber was signalled, recognized, surrounded. Fragoso had no big box, nor drum, nor cornet to attract the attention of his clients—not even a carriage of shining copper, with resplendent lamps and ornamented glass panels, nor a huge parasol, nor anything whatever to impress the public, as they generally have at fairs. No; but Fragoso had

his cup and ball, and how that cup and ball were manipu-
lated between his fingers! With what address did he
receive the turtle's head, which did for the ball on the
pointed end of the stick! With what grace did he make
the ball describe some learned curve of which mathema-
ticians have not yet calculated the value—even those who
have determined the wondrous curve of "the dog who
follows his master!"

Every native was there—men, women, the old and the
young, in their nearly primitive costume, looking on with
all their eyes, listening with all their ears. The smiling
entertainer, half in Portuguese, half in Ticunian, favoured
them with his customary oration in a tone of the most
rollicking good-humour. What he said was what is said by
all the charlatans who place their services at the public
disposal, whether they be Spanish Figaros or French perru-
quiers. At the bottom the same self-possession, the same
knowledge of human weakness, the same description of
thread-bare witticisms, the same amusing dexterity, and, on
the part of the natives, the same wide-mouth astonishment,
the same curiosity, the same credulity as the simple folk
of the civilized world.

It followed, then, that ten minutes later the public were
completely won, and crowded round Fragoso, who was
installed in a "loja" of the place, a sort of serving-bar to
the inn.

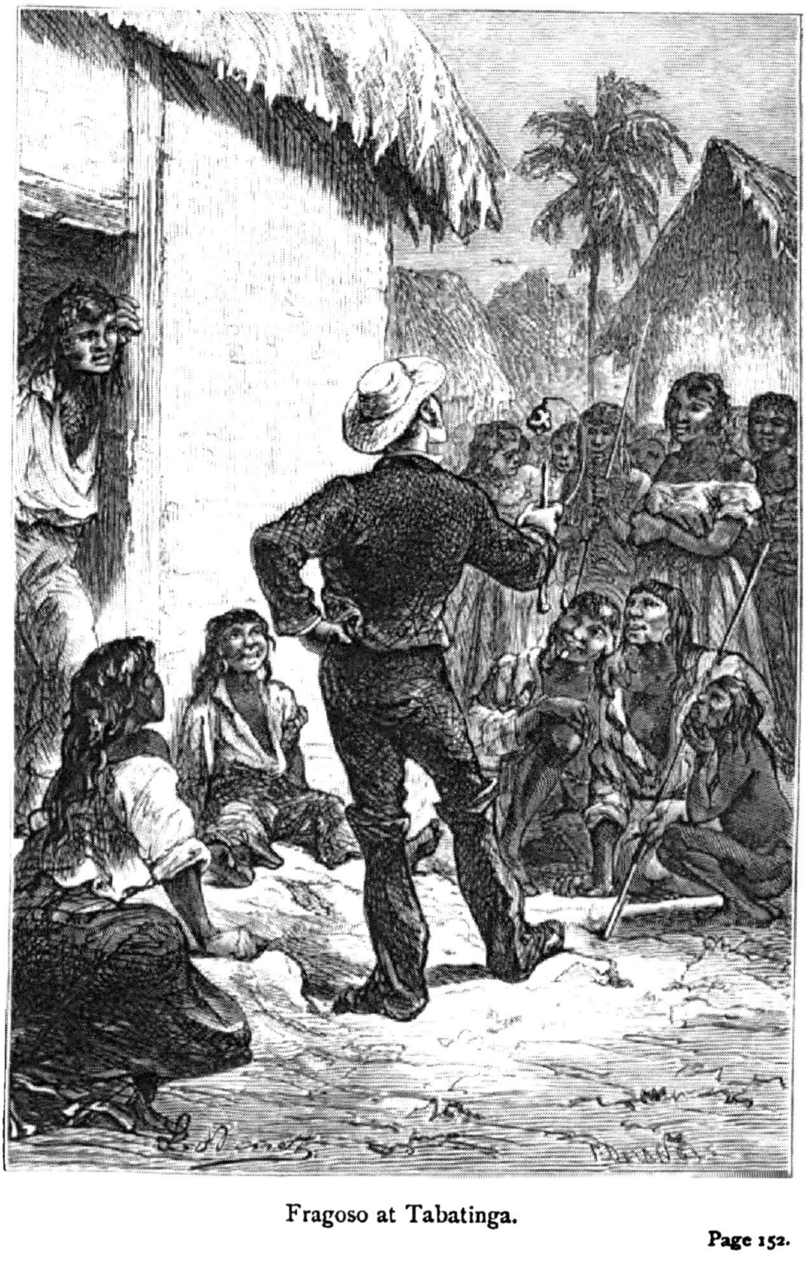

Fragoso at Tabatinga.

Page 152.

This loja belonged to a Brazilian settled at Tabatinga. There, for a few vatems, which are the sols of the country, and worth about twenty reis, or half a dozen centimes each, the natives could get drinks of the crudest, and particularly assai, a liquor half solid, half liquid, made of the fruits of the palm-tree, and drunk from a " cour," or half-calabash in general use in this district of the Amazon.

And then men and women, with equal eagerness, took their places on the barber's stool. The scissors of Fragoso had little to do, for it was not a question of cutting these wealthy heads of hair, nearly all remarkable for their softness and their quality, but the use to which he could put his comb and the tongs, which were kept warming in the corner in a brasier.

And then the encouragements of the artist to the crowd!

"Look here! look here!" said he; "how will that do, my friends—if you don't sleep on the top of it! There you are, for a twelvemonth! and these are the latest novelties from Belem and Rio de Janeiro! The Queen's maids of honour are not more cleverly decked out; and observe, I am not stingy with the pomade!"

No, he was not stingy with it. True, it was only a little grease, with which he had mixed some of the juices of a few flowers, but he plastered it on like cement!

And as to the names of the capillary edifices—for the

monuments reared by the hands of Fragoso were of every order of architecture—buckles, rings, clubs, tresses, crimpings, rolls, corkscrews, curls, everything found there a place. Nothing false ; no towers, no chignons, no shams! These heads were not enfeebled by cuttings nor thinned by fallings-off, but were forests in all their native virginity! Fragoso, however, was not above adding a few natural flowers, two or three long fish-bones, and some fine bone or copper ornaments, which were brought him by the dandies of the district. Assuredly, the exquisites of the Directory would have envied the arrangement of these high-art coiffures, three and four stories high, and the great Leonard himself would have bowed before his transatlantic rival.

And then the vatems, the handfuls of reis—the only coins for which the natives of the Amazon exchange their goods—which rained into the pocket of Fragoso, and which he collected with evident satisfaction. But assuredly night would come before he could satisfy the demands of the customers, who were so constantly renewed. It was not only the population of Tabatinga which crowded to the door of the loja. The news of the arrival of Fragoso was not slow to get abroad ; natives came to him from all sides : Ticunas from the left bank of the river, Mayorunas from the right bank, as well as those who live on the Cajuru and those who come from the villages of the Javary.

Waiting their turn.

Page 155.

A long array of anxious ones formed itself in the square. The happy ones coming from the hands of Fragoso went proudly from one house to another, showed themselves off, without daring to shake themselves, like the big children that they were.

It thus happened that when noon came the much-occupied barber had not had time to return on board, but had had to content himself with a little assai, some manioc flour, and turtle eggs, which he rapidly devoured between two applications of the curling-tongs.

But it was a great harvest for the innkeeper, as all the operations could not be conducted without a large absorption of liquors drawn from the cellars of the inn. In fact, it was an event for the town of Tabatinga, this visit of the celebrated Fragoso, barber in ordinary and extraordinary to the tribes of the Upper Amazon!

CHAPTER XIII.

TORRES.

AT five o'clock in the evening Fragoso was still there, and was asking himself if he would have to pass the night on the spot to satisfy the expectant crowd, when a stranger arrived in the square, and seeing all this native gathering, advanced towards the inn.

For some minutes the stranger eyed Fragoso attentively with some circumspection. The examination was obviously satisfactory, for he entered the loja.

He was a man about thirty-five years of age. He was dressed in a somewhat elegant travelling-costume, which added much to his personal appearance. But his strong black beard, which the scissors had not touched for some time, and his hair, a trifle long, imperiously required the good offices of a barber.

"Good-day, friend, good-day!" said he, lightly striking Fragoso on the shoulder.

Fragoso turned round when he heard the words pronounced in pure Brazilian, and not in the mixed idiom of the natives.

"A compatriot?" he asked, without stopping the twisting of the refractory mouth of a Mayouma head.

"Yes," answered the stranger. "A compatriot who has need of your services."

"To be sure! In a minute," said Fragoso. "Wait till I have finished with this lady!"

And this was done in a couple of strokes with the curling-tongs.

Although he was the last comer, and had no right to the vacant place, he sat down on the stool without causing any expostulation on the part of the natives who lost a turn.

Fragoso put down the irons for the scissors, and, after the manner of his brethren, said,—

"What can I do for you, sir?"

"Cut my beard and my hair," answered the stranger.

"All right!" said Fragoso, inserting his comb into the mass of hair.

And then the scissors to do their work.

"And you come from far?" asked Fragoso, who could not work without a good deal to say.

"I have come from the neighourhood of Iquitos."

"So have I!" exclaimed Fragoso. "I have come down the Amazon from Iquitos to Tabatinga. May I ask your name?"

"No objection at all," replied the stranger. " My name
is Torres."

When the hair was cut in the latest style Fragoso began to
thin his beard, but at this moment, as he was looking straight
into his face, he stopped, then began again, and then,—

"Eh! Mr. Torres," said he ; "I seem to know you. We
must have seen each other somewhere ? "

" I do not think so," quickly answered Torres.

" I am always wrong ! " replied Fragoso, and he hurried
on to finish his task.

A moment after Torres continued the conversation
which this question of Fragoso had interrupted, with,—

" How did you come from Iquitos ? "

" From Iquitos to Tabatinga ? "

" Yes."

" On board a raft, on which I was given a passage by a
worthy fazender who is going down the Amazon with his
family."

" A friend indeed ! " replied Torres.   " That is a chance
and if your fazender would take me—"

" Do you intend, then, to go down the river ? "

" Precisely."

" Into Para ? "

" No, only to Manaos, where I have business."

" Well, my host is very kind, and I think he would cheer-
fully oblige you."

Torres and Fragoso.

Page 159.

"Do you think so?"

"I might almost say I am sure."

"And what is the name of this fazender?" asked Torres carelessly.

"Joam Garral," answered Fragoso.

And at the same time he muttered to himself,—

"I certainly have seen this fellow somewhere!"

Torres was not the man to allow a conversation to drop which was likely to interest him, and for very good reasons.

"And so you think Joam Garral would give me a passage?"

"I do not doubt it," replied Fragoso. "What he would do for a poor chap like me he would not refuse to do for a compatriot like you."

"Is he alone on board the jangada?"

"No," replied Fragoso. "I was going to tell you that he is travelling with all his family—and jolly people they are, I assure you. He is accompanied by a crew of Indians and negroes, who form part of the staff at the fazenda."

"Is he rich?"

"Oh, certainly!" answered Fragoso—"very rich. Even the timber which forms the jangada, and the cargo it carries, constitute a fortune!"

"Then Joam Garral and his whole family have just passed the Brazilian frontier?"

"Yes," said Fragoso; "his wife, his son, his daughter, and Miss Minha's betrothed."

"Ah! he has a daughter?" said Torres.

"A charming girl!"

"Going to get married?"

"Yes, to a brave young fellow," replied Fragoso—"an army surgeon in garrison at Belem, and the wedding is to take place as soon as we get to the end of the voyage."

"Good!" said the smiling Torres; "it is what you might call a betrothal journey."

"A voyage of betrothal, of pleasure, and of business!" said Fragoso. "Madame Yaquita and her daughter have never set foot on Brazilian ground; and as for Joam Garral, it is the first time he has crossed the frontier since he went to the farm of old Magalhaes."

"I suppose," asked Torres, "that there are some servants with the family?"

"Of course," replied Fragoso—"old Cybele, on the farm for the last fifty years, and a pretty mulatto, Miss Lina, who is more of a companion than a servant to her mistress. Ah, what an amiable disposition! What a heart, and what eyes! And the ideas she has about everything, particularly about lianas—" Fragoso, started on this subject, would not have been able to stop himself, and Lina would have been the object of a good many enthusiastic declarations, had Torres not quitted the chair for another customer.

"What do I owe you?" asked he of the barber.

"Nothing," answered Fragoso. "Between compatriots, when they meet on the frontier, there can be no question of that sort."

"But," replied Torres, "I want to—"

"Very well, we will settle that later on, on board the jangada."

"But I do not know that, and I do not like to ask Joam Garral to allow me—"

"Do not hesitate!" exclaimed Fragoso; "I will speak to him if you would like it better, and he will be very happy to be of use to you under the circumstances."

And at that instant Manoel and Benito, coming into the town after dinner, appeared at the door of the loja, wishing to see Fragoso at work.

Torres turned towards them and suddenly said, "There are two gentlemen I know—or rather I remember."

"You remember them!" asked Fragoso, surprised.

"Yes, undoubtedly! A month ago, in the forest of Iquitos, they got me out of a considerable difficulty."

"But they are Benito Garral and Manoel Valdez."

"I know. They told me their names, but I never expected to see them here."

Torres advanced towards the two young men, who looked at him without recognizing him.

"You do not remember me, gentlemen?" he asked.

M

"Wait a little," answered Benito; "Mr. Torres, if I remember aright; it was you who, in the forest of Iquitos, got into difficulties with a guariba?"

"Quite true, gentlemen," replied Torres. "For six weeks I have been travelling down the Amazon, and I have just crossed the frontier at the same time as you have."

"Very pleased to see you again," said Benito; "but you have not forgotten that you promised to come to the fazenda to my father?"

"I have not forgotten it," answered Torres.

"And you would have done better to have accepted my offer; it would have allowed you to have waited for our departure, rested from your fatigues, and descended with us to the frontier; so many days of walking saved."

"To be sure!" answered Torres.

"Our compatriot is not going to stop at the frontier," said Fragoso, "he is going on to Manaos."

"Well, then," replied Benito, "if you will come on board the jangada you will be well received, and I am sure my father will give you a passage."

"Willingly," said Torres; "and you will allow me to thank you in advance."

Manoel took no part in the conversation; he let Benito make the offer of his services, and attentively watched Torres, whose face he scarcely remembered. There was an entire want of frankness in the eyes, whose look changed unceasingly, as if he was afraid to fix them anywhere. But Manoel kept this impression to himself, not wishing to injure a compatriot whom they were about to oblige.

"Gentlemen," said Torres, "if you like, I am ready to follow you to the landing-place."

"Come, then," answered Benito.

A quarter of an hour afterwards Torres was on board the jangada. Benito introduced him to Joam Garral, acquainting him with the circumstances under which they had previously met him, and asked him to give him a passage down to Manaos.

"I am happy, sir, to be able to oblige you," replied Joam.

"Thank you," said Torres, who at the moment of putting forth his hand kept it back in spite of himself.

"We shall be off at daybreak to-morrow," added Joam Garral, "so you had better get your things on board."

"Oh, that will not take me long!" answered Torres "there is only myself and nothing else!"

"Make yourself at home," said Joam Garral.

That evening Torres took possession of a cabin near to that of the barber. It was not till eight o'clock that the latter returned to the raft, and gave the young mulatto an account of his exploits, and repeated, with no little vanity, that the renown of the illustrious Fragoso was increasing in the basin of the Upper Amazon.

CHAPTER XIV.

STILL DESCENDING.

At daybreak on the morrow, the 27th of June, the cables were cast off, and the raft continued its journey down the river.

An extra passenger was on board. Whence came this Torres? No one exactly knew. Where was he going to? "To Manaos," he said. Torres was careful to let no suspicion of his past life escape him, nor of the profession that he had followed till within the last two months, and no one would have thought that the jangada had given refuge to an old captain of the woods. Joam Garral did not wish to mar the service he was rendering by questions of too pressing a nature.

In taking him on board the fazender had obeyed a sentiment of humanity. In the midst of these vast Amazonian deserts, more especially at the time when the steamers had not begun to furrow the waters, it was very difficult to find means of safe and rapid transit. Boats did not ply regularly, and in most cases the traveller was

obliged to walk across the forests. This is what Torres had
done, and what he would continue to have done, and it
was for him unexpected good luck to have got a passage on
the raft.

From the moment that Benito had explained under what
conditions he had met Torres the introduction was complete,
and he was able to consider himself as a passenger on an
Atlantic steamer, who is free to take part in the general
life if he cares, or free to keep himself a little apart if of an
unsociable disposition.

It was noticed, at least during the first few days, that
Torres did not try to become intimate with the Garral family.
He maintained a good deal of reserve, answering if addressed,
but never provoking a reply.

If he appeared more open with any one, it was with
Fragoso. Did he not owe to this gay companion the idea
of taking passage on board the raft? Many times he
asked him about the position of the Garrals at Iquitos, the
sentiments of the daughter for Manoel Valdez, and always
discreetly. Generally, when he was not walking alone in
the bow of the jangada, he kept to his cabin.

He breakfasted and dined with Joam Garral and his
family, but he took little part in their conversation, and
retired when the repast was finished.

During the morning the raft passed by the picturesque
group of islands situated in the vast estuary of the Javary.

This important affluent of the Amazon comes from the
south-west, and from source to mouth has not a single
island, nor a single rapid, to check its course. The mouth
is about three thousand feet in width, and the river comes in
some miles above the site formerly occupied by the town
of the same name, whose possession was disputed for so long
by Spaniards and Portuguese.

Up to the morning of the 30th of June there had been
nothing particular to distinguish the voyage. Occasionally
they met a few vessels gliding along by the banks attached
one to another in such a way that a single Indian could
manage the whole—" navigar de bubina," as this kind of
navigation is called by the people of the country, that is to
say, " confidence navigation."

They had soon passed the island of Araria, the Archipelago of the Calderon islands, the island of Capiatu, and
many others, whose names have not yet come to the
knowledge of geographers.

On the 30th of June the pilot signalled on the right the
little village of Jurupari-Tapera, where they halted for
two or three hours.

Manoel and Benito had gone shooting in the neighbourhood, and brought back some feathered game, which was
well received in the larder. At the same time they had
got an animal of whom a naturalist would have made more
than did the cook.

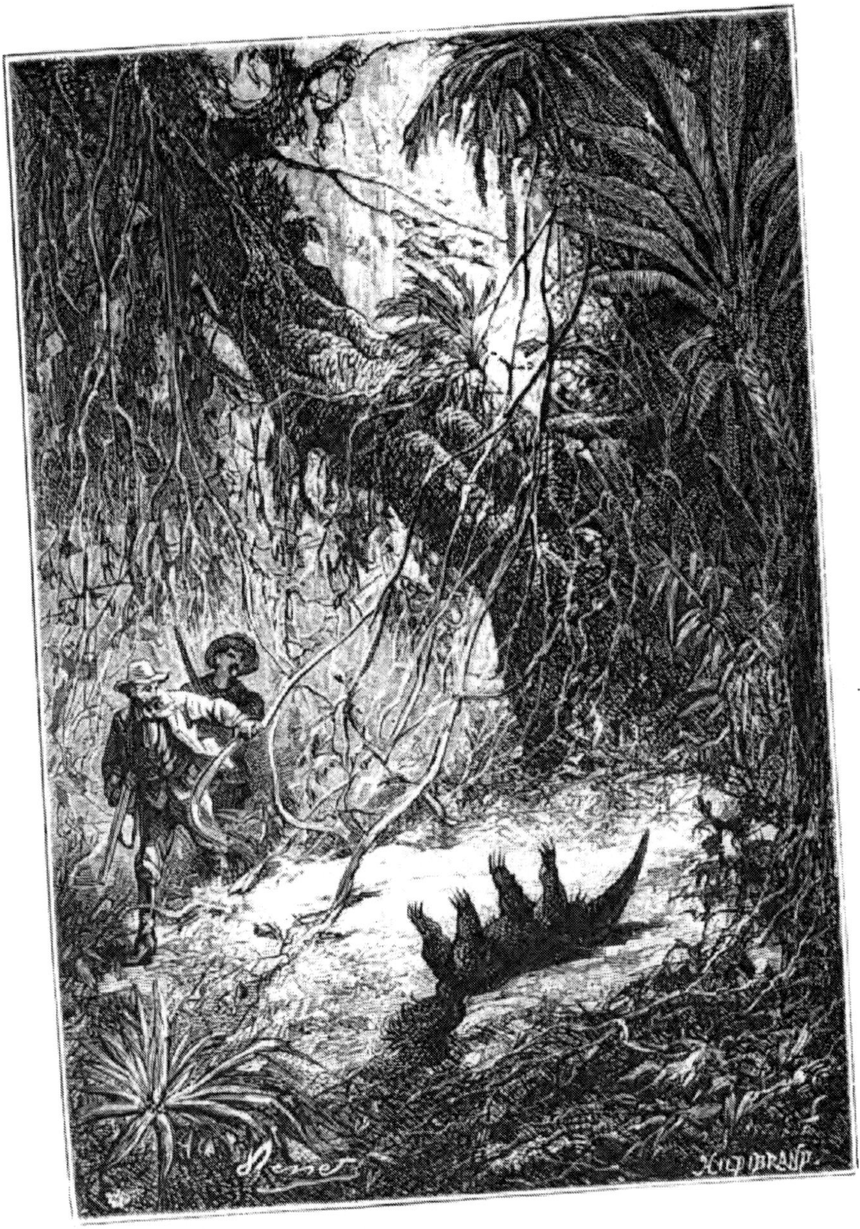
HILDIBRAND

The ant-eater. Page 167.

It was a creature of a dark colour, something like a large Newfoundland dog.

"A great ant-eater!" exclaimed Benito, as he threw it on the deck of the jangada.

"And a magnificent specimen, which would not disgrace the collection of a museum!" added Manoel.

"Did you take much trouble to catch the curious animal?" asked Minha.

"Yes, little sister," replied Benito, "and you were not there to ask for mercy! These dogs die hard, and no less than three bullets were necessary to bring this fellow down."

The ant-eater looked superb, with his long tail and grizzly hair, with his pointed snout which is plunged into the ant-hills whose insects form its principal food, and his long thin paws, armed with sharp nails, five inches long, and which can shut up like the fingers of one's hand. But what a hand was this hand of the ant-eater! When it has got hold of anything you have to cut it off to make it let go! It is of this hand that the traveller Emile Carrey has so justly observed, "the tiger himself would perish in its grasp."

On the 2nd of July, in the morning, the jangada arrived at the foot of San Pablo d'Olivença, after having floated through the midst of numerous islands which, in all seasons, are clad with verdure and shaded with magnificent trees, and the chief of which bear the names of Jurupari, Rita, Maracanatena, and Cururu Sapo. Many times they passed by the mouths of iguarapes, or little affluents, with black waters.

The coloration of these waters is a very curious phenomenon. It is peculiar to a certain number of these tributaries of the Amazon, which differ greatly in importance.

Manoel remarked how thick the cloudiness was, for it could be clearly seen on the surface of the whitish waters of the river.

"They have tried to explain this colouring in many ways," said he, "but I do not think the most learned have yet arrived at a satisfactory explanation."

"The waters are really black with a magnificent reflection of gold," replied Minha, showing a light reddish-brown cloth, which was floating level with the jangada.

"Yes," said Manoel, "and Humboldt has already observed the curious reflection that you have; but on looking at it attentively you will see that it is rather the colour of sepia which pervades the whole."

"Good!" exclaimed Benito. "Another phenomenon on which the *savants* are not agreed!"

"Perhaps," said Fragoso, "they might ask the opinion of the caymans, dolphins, and manatees, for they

The black water.

Page 169.

certainly prefer the black waters to the others to enjoy themselves in."

"They are particularly attractive to those animals," replied Manoel, but why it is rather embarrassing to say. For instance, is the coloration due to the hydro-carbons which the waters hold in solution, or is it because they flow through districts of peat, coal, and anthracite ; or should we not rather attribute it to the enormous quantity of minute plants which they bear along ? There is nothing certain in the matter. Under any circumstances, they are excellent to drink, of a freshness quite enviable for the climate, and without after-taste, and perfectly harmless. Take a little of the water, Minha, and drink it ; you will find it all right."

The water is in truth limpid and fresh, and would advantageously replace many of the table-waters used in Europe. They drew several frasques for kitchen use.

It has been said that in the morning of the 2nd of July the jangada had arrived at San Pablo d'Olivença, where they turn out in thousands those long strings of beads which are made from the scales of the "coco de piassaba." This trade is here extensively followed. It may, perhaps, seem singular that the ancient lords of the country, Tupinambas and Tupiniquis, should find their principal occupation in making objects for the Catholic religion. But after all, why not ? These Indians are no longer the Indians of days gone

by. Instead of being clothed in the national fashion, with
a frontlet of macaw feathers, bow, and blow-tube, have they
not adopted the American costume of white cotton trousers,
and a cotton poncho woven by their wives, who have become
thorough adepts in its manufacture?

San Pablo d'Olivença, a town of some importance, has
not less than two thousand inhabitants, derived from all the
neighbouring tribes. At present the capital of the Upper
Amazon, it began as a simple Mission, founded by the
Portuguese Carmelites about 1692, and afterwards acquired
by the Jesuit missionaries.

From the beginning it has been in the country of the
Omaguas, whose name means " flat-heads," and is derived
from the barbarous custom of the native mothers of squeezing
the heads of their new-born children between two plates, so
as to give them an oblong skull, which was then the fashion.
Like everything else, that has changed; heads have retaken
their natural form, and there is not the slightest trace of
the ancient deformity in the skulls of the chaplet-
makers.

Every one, with the exception of Joam Garral, went ashore.
Torres also remained on board, and showed no desire to
visit San Pablo d'Olivença, which he did not, however, seem
to be acquainted with.

Assuredly if the adventurer was taciturn he was not
inquisitive.

Benito had no difficulty in doing a little bartering, and adding slightly to the cargo of the jangada. He and the family received an excellent reception from the principal authorities of the town, the commandant of the place, and the chief of the custom-house, whose functions did not in the least prevent them from engaging in trade. They even entrusted the young merchant with a few products of the country for him to dispose of on their account at Manaos and Belem.

The town is composed of some sixty houses, arranged on the plain which hereabouts crowns the river-bank. Some of the huts are covered with tiles—a very rare thing in these countries; but, on the other hand, the humble church, dedicated to St. Peter and St. Paul, has only a roof of straw, rather more appropriate for a stable of Bethlehem than for an edifice consecrated to religion in one of the most Catholic countries of the world.

The commandant, his lieutenant, and the head of the police, accepted an invitation to dine with the family, and they were received by Joam Garral with the respect due to their rank.

During dinner Torres showed himself more talkative than usual. He spoke about some of his excursions into the interior of Brazil like a man who knew the country. But in speaking of these travels Torres did not neglect to ask the commandant if he knew Manaos, if his colleague would

be there at this time, and if the judge, the first magistrate
of the province, was accustomed to absent himself at this
period of the hot season.   It seemed that in putting this
series of questions Torres looked at Joam Garral.   It was
marked enough for even Benito to notice it, not without
surprise, and he observed that his father gave particular
attention to the questions so curiously propounded by
Torres.

The commandant of San Pablo d'Olivença assured the
adventurer that the authorities were not now absent from
Manaos, and he even asked Joam Garral to convey to them
his compliments.   In all probability the raft would arrive
before the town in seven weeks, or a little later, say about
the 20th or 25th of August.

The guests of the fazender took leave of the Garral
family towards the evening, and the following morning,
that of the 3rd of July, the jangada recommenced its descent
of the river.

At noon they passed on the left the mouth of the Yacu-
rupa.   This tributary, properly speaking, is a true canal, for
it discharges its waters into the Iça, which is itself an affluent
of the Amazon.

A peculiar phenomenon for the river in places itself to
feed its own tributaries !

Towards three o'clock in the afternoon the giant raft
passed the mouth of the Jandiatuba, which brings its

magnificent black waters from the south-west, and discharges them into the main artery by a mouth of four hundred metres in extent, after having watered the territories of the Culino Indians.

A number of islands were breasted—Pimaicaira, Caturia, Chico, Motachina ; some inhabited, others deserted, but all covered with superb vegetation, which forms an unbroken garland of green from one end of the Amazon to the other.

CHAPTER XV.

THE CONTINUED DESCENT.

ON the evening of the 5th of July, the atmosphere had been oppressive since the morning, and threatened approaching storms. Large bats of ruddy colour skimmed with their huge wings the current of the Amazon. Among them could be distinguished the "perros voladors," sombre brown above and light-coloured beneath, for which Minha, and particularly the young mulatto, felt an instinctive aversion.

These were, in fact, the horrible vampires which suck the blood of the cattle, and even attack man if he is imprudent enough to sleep out in the fields.

"Oh, the dreadful creatures!" cried Lina, hiding her eyes; "they fill me with horror!"

"And they are really formidable," added Minha; "are they not, Manoel?"

"To be sure—very formidable," answered he. "These vampires have a particular instinct which leads them to bleed you in the places where the blood most easily comes, and principally behind the ear. During the operation they continue to move their wings, and cause an agreeable freshness which renders the sleep of the sleeper more profound. They tell of people, unconsciously submitted to this hæmorrhage for many hours, who have never awoke!"

"Talk no more of things like that, Manoel," said Yaquita, "or neither Minha nor Lina will dare to sleep to-night."

"Never fear!" replied Manoel; "if necessary, we will watch over them as they sleep."

"Silence!" said Benito.

"What is the matter?" asked Manoel.

"Do you not hear a very curious noise on that side?" continued Benito, pointing to the right bank.

"Certainly," answered Yaquita.

"What causes the noise?" asked Minha. "One would think it was shingle rolling on the beach of the islands."

"Good! I know what it is," answered Benito. "To-morrow, at daybreak, there will be a rare treat for those who like fresh turtle eggs and little turtles!"

He was not deceived; the noise was produced by innumerable chelonians of all sizes, who were attracted to the islands to lay their eggs.

It is in the sand of the beach that these amphibians

choose the most convenient places to deposit their eggs. The operation commences with sunset and finishes with the dawn.

At this moment the chief turtle had left the bed of the river to reconnoitre for a favourable spot; the others, collected in thousands, were soon after occupied in digging with their hind paddles a trench six hundred feet long, a dozen wide, and six deep. After laying their eggs they cover them with a bed of sand, which they beat down with their carapaces as if they were rammers.

This egg-laying operation is a grand affair for the riverine Indians of the Amazon and its tributaries. They watch for the arrival of the chelonians, and proceed to the extraction of the eggs to the sound of the drum; and the harvest is divided into three parts—one to the watchers, another to the Indians, a third to the State, represented by the captains of the shore, who, in their capacity of police, have to superintend the collection of the dues. To certain beaches which the decrease of the waters has left uncovered, and which have the privilege of attracting the greater number of turtles, there has been given the name of "royal beaches." When the harvest is gathered it is a holiday for the Indians, who give themselves up to games, dancing, and drinking; and it is also a holiday for the alligators of the river, who hold high revelry on the remains of the amphibians.

Turtles, or turtle eggs, are an object of very considerable trade throughout the Amazonian basin. It is these chelonians whom they "turn"—that is to say, put on their backs—when they come from laying their eggs, and whom they preserve alive, keeping them in palisaded pools like fish-pools, or attaching them to a stake by a cord just long enough to allow them to go and come on the land or under the water. In this way they always have the meat of these animals fresh.

They proceed differently with the little turtles which are just hatched. There is no need to pack them or tie them up. Their shell is still soft, their flesh extremely tender, and after they have cooked them they eat them just like oysters. In this form large quantities are consumed.

However, this is not the most general use to which the chelonian eggs are put in the provinces of Amazones and Para. The manufacture of "manteigna de tartaruga," or turtle butter, which will bear comparison with the best products of Normandy or Brittany, does not take less every year than from two hundred and fifty to three hundred millions of eggs. But the turtles are innumerable all along the river, and they deposit their eggs on the sands of the beach in incalculable quantities. However, on account of the destruction caused not only by the natives, but by the water-fowl from the side, the urubus in the air, and the alligators in the river, their number has been so diminished

N

that for every little turtle a Brazilian pataque, or about a franc, has to be paid.

On the morrow, at daybreak, Benito, Fragoso, and a few Indians took a pirogue and landed on the beach of one of the large islands which they had passed during the night. It was not necessary for the jangada to halt. They knew they could catch her up.

On the shore they saw the little hillocks which indicated the places where, that very night, each packet of eggs had been deposited in the trench in groups of from one hundred and sixty to one hundred and ninety. These there was no wish to get out. But an earlier laying had taken place two months before, the eggs had hatched under the action of the heat stored in the sands, and already several thousands of little turtles were running about the beach.

The hunters were therefore in luck. The pirogue was filled with these interesting amphibians, and they arrived just in time for breakfast. The booty was divided between the passengers and crew of the jangada, and if any lasted till the evening it did not last any longer.

In the morning of the 7th of July they were before San Jose de Matura, a town situated near a small river filled up with long grass, and on the borders of which a legend says that Indians with tails once existed.

In the morning of the 8th of July they caught sight of the village of San Antonio, two or three little houses lost

Turtle-hunting.

Page 178.

in the trees at the mouth of the Iça, or Putumayo, which is about nine hundred metres wide.

The Putumayo is one of the most important affluents of the Amazon. Here in the sixteenth century missions were founded by the Spaniards, which were afterwards destroyed by the Portuguese, and not a trace of them now remains.

Representatives of different tribes of Indians are found in the neighbourhood, which are easily recognizable by the differences in their tattoo marks.

The Iça is a body of water coming from the east of the Pasto mountains to the north-east of Quito, through the finest forests of wild cacao-trees. Navigable for a distance of a hundred and forty leagues for steamers of not greater draught than six feet, it may one day become one of the chief waterways in the west of America.

The bad weather was at last met with. It did not show itself in continual rains, but in frequent storms. These could not hinder the progress of the raft, which offered little resistance to the wind. Its great length rendered it almost insensible to the swell of the Amazon, but during the torrential showers the Garral family had to keep indoors. They had to occupy profitably these hours of leisure. They chatted together, communicated their observations, and their tongues were seldom idle.

It was under these circumstances that little by little

Torres had begun to take a more active part in the conversation. The details of his many voyages throughout the whole north of Brazil afforded him numerous subjects to talk about. The man had certainly seen a great deal, but his observations were those of a sceptic, and he often shocked the straightforward people who were listening to him. It should be said that he showed himself much impressed towards Minha. But these attentions, although they were displeasing to Manoel, were not sufficiently marked for him to interfere. On the other hand, Minha felt for him an instinctive repulsion which she was at no pains to conceal.

On the 9th of July the mouth of the Tunantins appeared on the left bank, forming an estuary of some 400 feet across, in which it pours its blackish waters, coming from the west-north-west, after having watered the territories of the Cacena Indians. At this spot the Amazon appears under a truly grandiose aspect, but its course is more than ever encumbered with islands and islets. It required all the address of the pilot to steer through the archipelago, going from one bank to another, avoiding the shallows, shirking the eddies, and maintaining the advance.

They might have taken the Ahuaty Parana, a sort of natural canal, which goes off a little below the mouth of the Tunantins, and re-enters the principal stream a hundred and twenty miles farther on by the Rio Japura; but if the larger portion of this " furo " measures a hundred and fifty feet across, the narrowest is only sixty feet, and the raft would there have met with a difficulty.

On the 13th of July, after having touched at the island of Capuro, passed the mouth of the Jutahy, which, coming from the east-south-east, brings in its black waters by a mouth 500 feet wide, and admired the legions of monkeys, sulphur-white in colour with cinnabar-red faces, who are insatiable lovers of the nuts produced by the palm-trees from which the river derives its name, the travellers arrived on the 18th of July before the little village of Fonteboa.

At this place the jangada halted for twelve hours, so as to give a rest to the crew.

Fonteboa, like most of the mission villages of the Amazon, has not escaped the capricious fate which, during a lengthened period, moves them about from one place to the other. Probably the hamlet has now finished with its nomadic existence, and has definitely become stationary. So much the better ; for it is a charming place, with its thirty houses covered with foliage, and its church dedicated to Notre Dame de Guadaloupe, the Black Virgin of Mexico. Fonteboa has 1000 inhabitants, drawn from the Indians on both banks, who rear numerous cattle in the fields in the neighbourhood. These occupations do not end here, for they are intrepid hunters, or, if they prefer it, intrepid fishers for the manatee.

On the evening of their arrival the young fellows assisted at a very interesting expedition of this nature. Two of these herbivorous cetaceans had just been signalled in the black waters of the Cayaratu, which comes in at Fonteboa. Six brown points were seen moving along the surface, and these were the two pointed snouts and four pinions of the lamantins.

Inexperienced fishermen would at first have taken these moving points for floating wreckage, but the natives of Fonteboa were not to be so deceived. Besides, very soon loud blowings indicated that the spouting animals were vigorously ejecting the air which had become useless for their breathing purposes.

Two ubas, each carrying three fishermen, set off from the bank and approached the manatees, who soon took flight. The black points at first traced a long furrow on the top of the water, and then disappeared for a time.

The fishermen continued their cautious advance. One of them, armed with a very primitive harpoon—a long nail at the end of a stick—kept himself in the bow of the boat, while the other two noiselessly paddled on. They waited till the necessity of breathing would bring the manatees up again. In ten minutes or thereabouts the animals would certainly appear in a circle more or less confined.

In fact, this time had scarcely elapsed before the black

The manatees.

Page 183.

points emerged at a little distance, and two jets of air mingled with vapour were noisily shot forth.

The ubas approached, the harpoons were thrown at the same instant; one missed its mark, but the other struck one of the cetaceans near his tail.

It was only necessary to stun the animal, who rarely defends himself when touched by the iron of the harpoon. In a few pulls the cord brought him alongside the uba, and he was towed to the beach at the foot of the village.

It was not a manatee of any size, for it only measured about three feet long. These poor cetaceans have been so hunted that they have become very rare in the Amazon and its affluents, and so little time is left them to grow that the giants of the species do not now exceed seven feet. What are these, after manatees twelve and fifteen feet long, which still abound in the rivers and lakes of Africa?

But it would be difficult to hinder their destruction. The flesh of the manatee is excellent, superior even to that of pork, and the oil furnished by its lard, which is three inches thick, is a product of great value. When the meat is smoke-dried it keeps for a long time, and is capital food. If to this is added that the animal is easily caught, it is not to be wondered at that the species is on its way to complete destruction.

On the 19th of July, at sunrise, the jangada left Fonteboa,

and entered between the two completely deserted banks
of the river, and breasted some islands shaded with the
grand forests of cacao-trees. The sky was heavily charged
with electric cumuli, warning them of renewed storms.

The Rio Jurua, coming from the south-west, soon joins
the river on the left. A vessel can go up it into Peru
without encountering insurmountable obstacles among its
white waters, which are fed by a great number of petty
affluents.

"It is perhaps in these parts," said Manoel, "that we
ought to look for those female warriors who so much astonished Orellana. But we ought to say that, like their
predecessors, they do not form separate tribes; they are
simply the wives who accompany their husbands to the
fight, and who, among the Juruas, have a great reputation
for bravery."

The jangada continued to descend; but what a labyrinth the Amazon now appeared ! The Rio Japura, whose
mouth was forty-eight miles on ahead, and which is one
of its largest tributaries, runs almost parallel with the
river.

Between them were canals, iguarapes, lagoons, temporary
lakes, an inextricable network which renders the hydro-
graphy of this country so difficult.

But if Araujo had no map to guide him, his experience
served him more surely, and it was wonderful to see him

unravelling the chaos, without ever turning aside from the main river.

In fact, he did so well that on the 25th of July, in the afternoon, after having passed before the village of Parani-Tapera, the raft was anchored at the entrance of the Lake of Ega, or Teffe, which it was useless to enter, for they would not have been able to get out of it again into the Amazon.

But the town of Ega is of some importance; it was worthy of a halt to visit it. It was arranged, therefore, that the jangada should remain on this spot till the 27th of July, and that on the morrow the large pirogue should take the whole family to Ega. This would give a rest, which was deservedly due to the hard-working crew of the raft.

The night passed at the moorings near a slightly rising shore, and nothing disturbed the quiet. A little sheet-lightning was observable on the horizon, but it came from a distant storm which did not reach the entrance to the lake

CHAPTER XVI.

EGA.

AT six o'clock in the morning of the 20th of July, Yaquita, Minha, Lina, and the two young men prepared to leave the jangada.

Joam Garral, who had shown no intention of putting his foot on shore, had decided this time, at the request of the ladies of his family, to leave his absorbing daily work and accompany them on their excursion. Torres had evinced no desire to visit Ega, to the great satisfaction of Manoel, who had taken a great dislike to the man, and only waited for an opportunity to declare it.

As to Fragoso, he could not have the same reason for going to Ega as had taken him to Tabatinga, which is a place of little importance compared to this.

Ega is a chief town with fifteen hundred inhabitants, and in it reside all those authorities which compose the administration of a considerable city—considerable for the country; that is to say, the military commandant, the chief of the police, the judges, the schoolmaster, and troops under the command of officers of all ranks.

With so many functionaries living in a town, with their wives and children, it is easy to see that hairdressers would be in demand. Such was the case, and Fragoso would not have paid his expenses.

Doubtless, however, the jolly fellow, who could do no business in Ega, had thought to be of the party if Lina went with her mistress, but, just as they were leaving the raft, he resolved to remain, at the request of Lina herself.

"Mr. Fragoso!" she said to him, after taking him aside.

"Miss Lina?" answered Fragoso.

"I do not think that your friend Torres intends to go with us to Ega."

"Certainly not, he is going to stay on board, Miss Lina, but you would oblige me by not calling him my friend!"

"But you undertook to ask a passage for him before he had shown any intention of doing so."

"Yes, and on that occasion, if you would like to know what I think, I made a fool of myself!"

"Quite so! and if you would like to know what I think, I do not like the man at all, Mr. Fragoso."

"Neither do I, Miss Lina, and I have all the time an idea that I have seen him somewhere before. But the remembrance is too vague; the impression, however, is far from being a pleasant one!"

"Where and when could you have met him? Cannot you call it to mind? It might be useful to know who he is and what he has been."

"No—I try all I can. How long was it ago? In what country? Under what circumstances? And I cannot hit upon it."

"Mr. Fragoso!"

"Miss Lina!"

"Stay on board and keep watch on Torres during our absence!"

"What? Not go with you to Ega, and remain a whole day without seeing you!"

"I ask you to do so!"

"Is it an order?"

"It is an entreaty!"

"I will remain!"

"Mr. Fragoso!"

"Miss Lina!"

"I thank you!"

"Thank me, then, with a good shake of the hand," replied Fragoso, "that is worth something!"

Lina held out her hand, and Fragoso kept it for a few moments while he looked into her face. And that is the reason why he did not take his place in the pirogue,

The landing on the beach.

Page 189.

and became, without appearing to be, the guard upon Torres.

Did the latter notice the feelings of aversion with which he was regarded? Perhaps, but doubtless he had his reasons for taking no account of them.

A distance of four leagues separated the mooring-place from the town of Ega. Eight leagues, there and back, in a pirogue containing six persons, besides two negroes as rowers, would take some hours, not to mention the fatigue caused by the high temperature, though the sky was veiled with clouds.

Fortunately a lovely breeze blew from the north-west, and if it held would be favourable for crossing Lake Teffe. They could go to Ega and return rapidly without having to tack.

So the lateen sail was hoisted on the mast of the pirogue. Benito took the tiller, and off they went, after a last gesture from Lina to Fragoso to keep his eyes open.

The southern shore of the lake had to be followed to get to Ega.

After two hours the pirogue arrived at the port of this ancient mission, founded by the Carmelites, which became a town in 1759, and which General Gama placed for ever under Brazilian rule.

The passengers landed on a flat beach, on which were to

be found not only boats from the interior, but a few of those little schooners which are used in the coasting-trade on the Atlantic seaboard.

When the two girls entered Ega they were at first much astonished.

"What a large town!" said Minha.

"What houses! what people!" replied Lina, whose eyes seemed to have expanded so that she might see better.

"Rather!" said Benito laughingly. "More than fifteen hundred inhabitants! Two hundred houses at the very least! Some of them with a first floor! And two or three streets! Genuine streets!"

"My dear Manoel!" said Minha, "do protect us against my brother! He is making fun of us, and only because he has already been in the finest towns in Amazones and Para!"

"Quite so, and he is also poking fun at his mother," added Yaquita, "for I confess I never saw anything equal to this!"

"Then, mother and sister, you must take great care that you do not fall into a trance when you get to Manaos, and vanish altogether when you reach Belem!"

"Never fear," answered Manoel, "the ladies will have been gently prepared for these grand wonders by visiting the principal cities of the Upper Amazon!"

"Now, Manoel," said Minha, "you are talking just like my brother! Are you making fun of us, too?"

"No, Minha, I assure you."

"Laugh on, gentlemen," said Lina, "and let us look around, my dear mistress, for it is very fine!"

Very fine! A collection of houses, built of mud, white-washed, and principally covered with thatch or palm-leaves; a few built of stone or wood, with verandahs, doors, and shutters painted a bright green, standing in the middle of a small orchard of orange-trees in flower. But there were two or three public buildings, a barrack, and a church dedicated to St. Theresa, which was a cathedral by the side of the modest chapel at Iquitos. On looking towards the lake a beautiful panorama unfolded itself, bordered by a frame of cocoa-nut trees and assais, which ended at the edge of the liquid level, and showed beyond the picturesque village of Noqueira, with its few small houses lost in the mass of the old olive-trees on the beach.

But for the two girls there was another cause of wonderment, quite feminine wonderment too, in the fashions of the fair Egans, not the primitive costume of the natives, converted Omaas or Muras, but the dress of true Brazilian ladies. The wives and daughters of the principal functionaries and merchants of the town pre-tentiously showed off their Parisian toilettes, a little out of date perhaps, for Ega is five hundred leagues away from Para, and this is itself many thousands of miles from Paris.

"Just look at those fine ladies in their fine clothes!"

"Lina will go mad!" exclaimed Benito.

"If those dresses were worn properly," said Minha, "they might not be so ridiculous!"

"My dear Minha," said Manoel, "with your simple gown and straw hat, you are better dressed than any one of these Brazilians, with their headgear and flying petticoats, which are foreign to their country and their race."

"If it pleases you to think so," answered Minha, "I do not envy any of them."

But they had come to see. They walked through the streets, which contained more stalls than shops ; they strolled about the market-place, the rendezvous of the fashionables, who were nearly stifled in their European clothes ; they even breakfasted at an hotel—it was scarcely an inn— whose cookery caused them to deeply regret the excellent service on the raft.

After dinner, at which only turtle flesh, served up in different forms, appeared, the Garral family went for the last time to admire the borders of the lake as the setting sun gilded it with its rays ; then they rejoined their pirogue, somewhat disillusionized perhaps as to the magnificence of a town which one hour would give time enough to visit,

After the dinner.

Page 192.

and a little tired with walking about its stifling streets which were not nearly so pleasant as the shady pathways of Iquitos. The inquisitive Lina's enthusiasm alone had not been damped.

They all took their places in the pirogue. The wind remained in the north-west, and had freshened with the evening. The sail was hoisted. They took the same course as in the morning, across the lake fed by the black waters of the Rio Teffe, which, according to the Indians, is navigable towards the south-west for forty days' journey. At eight o'clock the pirogue regained the mooring-place and hailed the jangada.

As soon as Lina could get Fragoso aside,—

"Have you seen anything suspicious?" she inquired.

"Nothing, Miss Lina," he replied; "Torres has scarcely left his cabin, where he has been reading and writing."

"He did not get into the house or the dining-room, as I feared?"

"No, all the time he was not in his cabin he was in the bow of the raft."

"And what was he doing?"

"Holding an old piece of paper in his hand, consulting it with great attention, and muttering a lot of incomprehensible words."

"All that is not so unimportant as you think, Mr. Fragoso! These readings and writings and old papers have

o

their interest! He is neither a professor nor a lawyer, this reader and writer!"

"You are right!"

"Still watch him, Mr. Fragoso!"

"I will watch him always, Miss Lina," replied Fragoso.

On the morrow, the 27th of July, at daybreak, Benito gave the pilot the signal to start.

Away between the islands, in the Bay of Arenapo, the mouth of the Japura, six thousand six hundred feet wide, was seen for an instant. This large tributary comes into the Amazon through eight mouths, as if it were pouring into some gulf or ocean. But its waters come from afar, and it is the mountains of the Republic of Ecuador which start them on a course that there are no falls to break until two hundred and ten leagues from its junction with the main stream.

All this day was spent in descending to the island of Yapura, after which the river, less interfered with, makes navigation much easier. The current is not so rapid and the islets are easily avoided, so that there were no touchings or groundings.

The next day the jangada coasted along by vast beaches formed by undulating high domes, which served as the barriers of immense pasture-grounds, in which the whole of the cattle in Europe could be raised and fed. These sandbanks are considered to be the richest turtle grounds in the basin of the Upper Amazon.

On the evening of the 29th of July they were securely moored off the island of Catua, so as to pass the night, which promised to be dark.

On this island, as soon as the sun rose above the horizon, there appeared a party of Muras Indians, the remains of that ancient and powerful tribe, which formerly occupied more than a hundred leagues of the river bank between the Teffe and the Madeira.

These Indians went and came, watching the raft, which remained stationary. There were about a hundred of them armed with blow-tubes formed of a reed peculiar to these parts, and which is strengthened outside by the stem of a dwarf palm from which the pith has been extracted.

Joam Garral quitted for an instant the work which took up all his time, to warn his people to keep a good guard and not to provoke these Indians.

In truth the sides were not well matched. The Muras are remarkably clever at sending through their blow-tubes arrows which cause incurable wounds, even at a range of three hundred paces.

These arrows, made of the leaf of the "coucourite" palm, are feathered with cotton, and nine or ten inches long, with a point like a needle, and poisoned with "curare."

Curare, or "wourah," the liquor "which kills in a whisper,"

as the Indians say, is prepared from the sap of one of the euphorbiaceæ and the juice of a bulbous strychnos, not to mention the paste of venomous ants and poisonous serpent fangs which they mix with it.

"It is indeed a terrible poison," said Manoel.   "It attacks at once those nerves by which the movements are subordinated to the will. But the heart is not touched, and it does not cease to beat until the extinction of the vital functions, and besides no antidote is known to the poison, which commences by numbness of the limbs."

Very fortunately, these Muras made no hostile demonstrations, although they entertain a profound hatred towards the whites. They have, in truth, no longer the courage of their ancestors.

At nightfall a five-holed flute was heard behind the trees in the island, playing several airs in a minor key.   Another flute answered.   This interchange of musical phrases lasted for two or three minutes, and the Muras disappeared.

Fragoso, in an exuberant moment, had tried to reply by a song in his own fashion, but Lina had clapped her hand on his mouth, and prevented his showing off his insignificant singing talents, which he was so willingly lavish of.

On the 2nd of August, at three o'clock in the afternoon, the raft arrived twenty leagues away from there at Lake Apoara, which is fed by the black waters of the river of the same name, and two days afterwards, about five o'clock, it stopped at the entrance into Lake Coary.

This lake is one of the largest which communicates with the Amazon, and it serves as a reservoir for different rivers. Five or six affluents run into it, are there stored and mixed up, and emerge by a narrow channel into the main stream.

After catching a glimpse of the hamlet of Tahua-Miri, mounted on its piles as on stilts, as a protection against inundation from the floods, which often sweep up over these low sandbanks, the raft was moored for the night.

The stoppage was made in sight of the village of Coary, a dozen houses, considerably dilapidated, built in the midst of a thick mass of orange and calabash trees.

Nothing can be more changeable than the aspect of this village, for according to the rise or fall of the water, the lake stretches away on all sides of it, or is reduced to a narrow canal, scarcely deep enough to communicate with the Amazon.

On the following morning, that of the 5th of August, they started at dawn, passing the canal of Yucura, belonging to the tangled system of lakes and furos of the Rio Zapura, and on the morning of the 6th of August they reached the entrance to Lake Miana.

No fresh incident occurred in the life on board, which proceeded with almost methodical regularity.

Fragoso, urged on by Lina, did not cease to watch Torres.

Many times he tried to get him to talk about his past life; but the adventurer eluded all conversation on the subject, and ended by maintaining a strict reserve towards the barber.

His intercourse with the Garral family remained the same. If he spoke little to Joam, he addressed himself more willingly to Yaquita and her daughter, and appeared not to notice the evident coolness with which he was received. They all agreed that when the raft arrived at Manaos, Torres should leave it, and that they would never speak of him again. Yaquita followed the advice of Padre Passanha, who counselled patience, but the good priest had not such an easy task in Manoel, who was quite disposed to put on shore the intruder who had been so unfortunately taken on to the raft.

The only thing that happened on this evening was the following.

A pirogue, going down the river, came alongside the jangada, after being hailed by Joam Garral.

"Are you going to Manaos?" asked he of the Indian who commanded and was steering her.

"Yes," replied he.

"When will you get there?"

"In eight days."

" Then you will arrive before we shall. Will you deliver a letter for me? "

" With pleasure."

" Take this letter, then, my friend, and deliver it at Manaos."

The Indian took the letter which Joam gave him, and a handful of reis was the price of the commission he had undertaken.

No members of the family, then gone into the house, knew anything of this. Torres was the only witness. He heard a few words exchanged between Joam and the Indian, and from the cloud which passed over his face it was easy to see that the sending of this letter considerably surprised him.

CHAPTER XVII.

AN ATTACK.

HOWEVER, if Manoel, to avoid giving rise to a violent scene on board, said nothing on the subject of Torres, he resolved to have an explanation with Benito.

"Benito," he began, after taking him to the bow of the jangada, "I have something to say to you."

Benito, generally so good-humoured, stopped as he looked at Manoel, and a cloud came over his countenance.

"I know why," he said; "it is about Torres."

"Yes, Benito."

"And I also wish to speak to you."

"You have then noticed his attention to Minha?" said Manoel, turning pale.

"Ah! It is not a feeling of jealousy, though, that exasperates you against such a man?" said Benito quickly.

"No!" replied Manoel. "Decidedly not! Heaven forbid I should do such an injury to the girl who is to become my wife. No, Benito! She holds the adventurer in horror! I am not thinking anything of that sort; but it distresses me to see this adventurer constantly obtruding himself by his presence and conversation on your mother and sister, and seeking to introduce himself into that intimacy with your family which is already mine."

"Manoel," gravely answered Benito, "I share your aversion for this dubious individual, and had I consulted my feelings, I would already have driven Torres off the raft! But I dare not!"

"You dare not?" said Manoel, seizing the hand of his friend. "You dare not?"

"Listen to me, Manoel," continued Benito. "You have observed Torres well, have you not? You have remarked his attentions to my sister! Nothing can be truer! But while you have been noticing that, have you not seen that this annoying man never keeps his eyes off my father, no matter if he is near to him or far from him, and that he seems to have some spiteful secret intention in watching him with such unaccountable persistency?"

"What are you talking about, Benito? Have you any reason to think that Torres bears some grudge against Joam Garrel?"

"No! I think nothing!" replied Benito, "it is only a presentiment! But look well at Torres, study his face with

care, and you will see what an evil grin he has whenever
my father comes into his sight."

"Well, then," exclaimed Manoel, "if it is so, Benito, the
more reason for clearing him out!"

"More reason—or less reason," replied Benito. "Manoel,
I fear—what? I know not—but to force my father to get
rid of Torres would perhaps be imprudent! I repeat it, I
am afraid, though no positive fact enables me to explain
my fear to myself!"

And Benito seemed to shudder with anger as he said
these words.

"Then," said Manoel, "you think we had better wait?"

"Yes; wait, before doing anything, but above all things
let us be on our guard!"

"After all," answered Manoel, "in twenty days we shall
be at Manaos. There Torres must stop. There he will
leave us, and we shall be relieved of his presence for good!
Till then we must keep our eyes on him!"

"You understand me, Manoel?" asked Benito.

"I understand you, my friend, my brother!" replied
Manoel, "although I do not share, and cannot share, your
fears! What connexion can possibly exist between your
father and this adventurer? Evidently your father has
never seen him!"

"I do not say that my father knows Torres," said Benito,
"but assuredly it seems to me that Torres knows my father.

What was the fellow doing in the neighbourhood of the fazenda when we met him in the forest of Iquitos? Why did he then refuse the hospitality which we offered, so as to afterwards manage to force himself on us as our travelling companion? We arrive at Tabatinga, and there he is as if he was waiting for us! The probability is that these meetings were in pursuance of a preconceived plan. When I see the shifty, dogged look of Torres, all this crowds on my mind. I do not know! I am losing myself in things that defy explanation! Oh! why did I ever think of offering to take him on board this raft?"

"Be calm, Benito, I pray you!"

"Manoel!" continued Benito, who seemed to be powerless to contain himself, "think you that if it only concerned me—this man who inspires us all with such aversion and disgust—I should hesitate to throw him overboard? But when it concerns my father, I fear lest in giving way to my impressions I may be injuring my object! Something tells me that with this scheming fellow there may be danger in doing anything until he has given us the right—the right and the duty—to do it. In short, on the jangada, he is in our power, and if we both keep good watch over my father, we can spoil his game, no matter how sure it may be, and force him to unmask and betray himself! Then wait a little longer!"

The arrival of Torres in the bow of the raft broke off

the conversation. Torres looked slyly at the two young men, but said not a word.

Benito was not deceived when he said that the adventurer's eyes were never off Joam Garral as long as he fancied he was unobserved.

No! he was not deceived when he said that Torres' face grew evil when he looked at his father!

By what mysterious bond could these two men—one nobleness itself, that was self-evident—be connected with each other?

Such being the state of affairs it was certainly difficult for Torres, constantly watched as he was by the two young men, by Fragoso and Lina, to make a single movement without having instantly to repress it. Perhaps he understood the position. If he did, he did not show it, for his manner changed not in the least.

Satisfied with their mutual explanation, Manoel and Benito promised to keep him in sight without doing anything to awaken his suspicions.

During the following days the jangada passed on the right the mouths of the rivers Camara, Aru, and Yuripari, whose waters instead of flowing into the Amazon run off to the south to feed the Rio des Purus, and return by it into the main river. At five o'clock on the evening of the 10th of August, they put into the island of Cocos.

They there passed a "seringal." This name is applied

Preparing caoutchouc.

Page 205.

to a caoutchouc plantation, the caoutchouc being extracted from the "seringueira" tree, whose scientific name is *siphonia elastica.*

It is said that by negligence or bad management, the number of these trees is decreasing in the basin of the Amazon, but the forests of seringueira-trees are still very considerable on the banks of the Madeira, Purus, and other tributaries.

There were here some twenty Indians collecting and working the caoutchouc, an operation which principally takes place during the months of May, June, and July.

After having ascertained that the trees, well prepared by the river floods which have bathed their stems to a height of about four feet, are in good condition for the harvest, the Indians set to work.

Incisions are made into the alburnum of the seringueiras ; below the wound small pots are attached, which twenty-four hours suffice to fill with a milky sap. It can also be collected by means of a hollow bamboo, and a receptacle placed on the ground at the foot of the tree.

The sap being obtained, the Indians, to prevent the separation of its peculiar resins, fumigate it over a fire of the nuts of the assai palm. By spreading out the sap on a wooden scoop, and shaking it in the smoke, its coagulation is almost immediately obtained ; it assumes a greyish yellow tinge and solidifies. The layers formed in succession are detached from the scoop, exposed to the sun, hardened, and assume the brownish colour with which we are familiar. The manufacture is then complete.

Benito, finding a capital opportunity, bought from the Indians all the caoutchouc stored in their cabins, which, by the way, are mostly built on piles. The price he gave them was sufficiently remunerative, and they were highly satisfied.

Four days later, on the 14th of August, the jangada passed the mouths of the Purus.

This is another of the large affluents of the Amazon, and seems to possess a navigable course, even for large ships, of over 500 leagues. It rises in the south-west, and measures nearly 5000 feet across at its junction with the main river. After winding beneath the shade of ficuses, tahuaris, nipa palms, and cecropias, it enters the Amazon by five mouths.

Hereabouts Araujo the pilot managed with great ease. The course of the river was but slightly obstructed with islands, and besides, from one bank to another its width is about two leagues.

The current, too, took along the jangada more steadily, and on the 18th of August it stopped at the village of Pasquero to pass the night.

The sun was already low on the horizon, and with the

rapidity peculiar to these low latitudes, was about to set vertically, like an enormous meteor.

Joam Garral and his wife, Lina, and old Cybele, were in front of the house.

Torres, after having for an instant turned towards Joam, as if he would speak to him, and prevented perhaps by the arrival of Padre Passanha, who had come to bid the family good-night, had gone back to his cabin.

The Indians and the negroes were at their quarters along the sides. Araujo, seated at the bow, was watching the current which extended straight away in front of him.

Manoel and Benito, with their eyes open, but chatting and smoking with apparent indifference, walked about the central part of the raft awaiting the hour of repose.

All at once Manoel stopped Benito with his hand and said,—

"What a queer smell! Am I wrong? Do you not notice it?"

"One would say that it was the odour of burning musk!" replied Benito. "There ought to be some alligators asleep on the neighbouring beach!"

"Well, Nature has done wisely in allowing them so to betray themselves."

"Yes," said Benito, "it is fortunate, for they are sufficiently formidable creatures!"

Often at the close of the day these saurians love to

stretch themselves on the shore, and instal themselves comfortably there to pass the night.   Crouched at the opening
of a hole, into which they have crept back, they sleep with
the mouth open, the upper jaw perpendicularly erect, so as
to lie in wait for their prey.   To these amphibians it is but
sport to launch themselves in its pursuit, either by swimming through the waters propelled by their tails or running
along the bank with a speed no man can equal.

It is on these huge beaches that the caymans are born,
live, and die, not without affording extraordinary examples
of longevity.   Not only can the old ones, the centenarians,
be recognized by the greenish moss which carpets their
carcass and is scattered over its protuberances, but by their
natural ferocity, which increases with age.   As Benito said,
they are formidable creatures, and it is fortunate that their
attacks can be guarded against.

Suddenly cries were heard in the bow.

"Caymans! caymans!"

Manoel and Benito came forward and looked.

Three large saurians, from fifteen to twenty feet
long, had managed to clamber on to the platform of the
raft.

"Bring the guns! Bring the guns!" shouted Benito,
making signs to the Indians and the blacks to get behind.

"Into the house!" said Manoel, "make haste!"

And in truth, as they could not attack them at once, the best thing they could do was to get into shelter without delay.

It was done in an instant. The Garral family took refuge in the house, where the two young men joined them. The Indians and the negroes ran into their huts and cabins. As they were shutting the door,—

"And Minha?" said Manoel.

"She is not there!" replied Lina, who had just run to her mistress's room.

"Good heavens! where is she?" exclaimed her mother, and they all shouted at once,—

"Minha! Minha!"

No reply.

"There she is on the bow of the jangada!" said Benito.

"Minha!" shouted Manoel.

The two young men, and Fragoso and Joam Garral, thinking no more of danger, rushed out of the house, guns in hand.

Scarcely were they outside when two of the alligators made a half-turn and ran towards them.

A dose of buckshot in the head, close to the eye, from Benito, stopped one of the monsters, who, mortally wounded, writhed in frightful convulsions and fell on his side.

But the second still lived, and came on, and there was no way of avoiding him.

P

The huge alligator tore up to Joam Garral, and after knocking him over with a sweep of his tail, ran at him with open jaws.

At this moment Torres rushed from the cabin, hatchet in hand, and struck such a terrific blow that its edge sunk into the jaw of the cayman and left him defenceless.

Blinded by the blood, the animal flew to the side and, designedly or not, fell over and was lost in the stream.

"Minha ! Minha !" shouted Manoel in distraction, when he got to the bow of the jangada.

Suddenly she came in view. She had taken refuge in the cabin of Araujo, and the cabin had just been upset by a powerful blow from the third alligator. Minha was flying aft, pursued by the monster, who was not six feet away from her.

Minha fell.

A second shot from Benito failed to stop the cayman. He only struck the animal's carapace, and the scales flew in splinters, but the ball did not penetrate.

Manoel threw himself at the girl to raise her, or to snatch her from death ! A side-blow from the animal's tail knocked him down too.

Minha fainted, and the mouth of the alligator opened to crush her !

And then Fragoso jumped on to the animal, and thrust in a knife to the very bottom of his throat, at the risk of

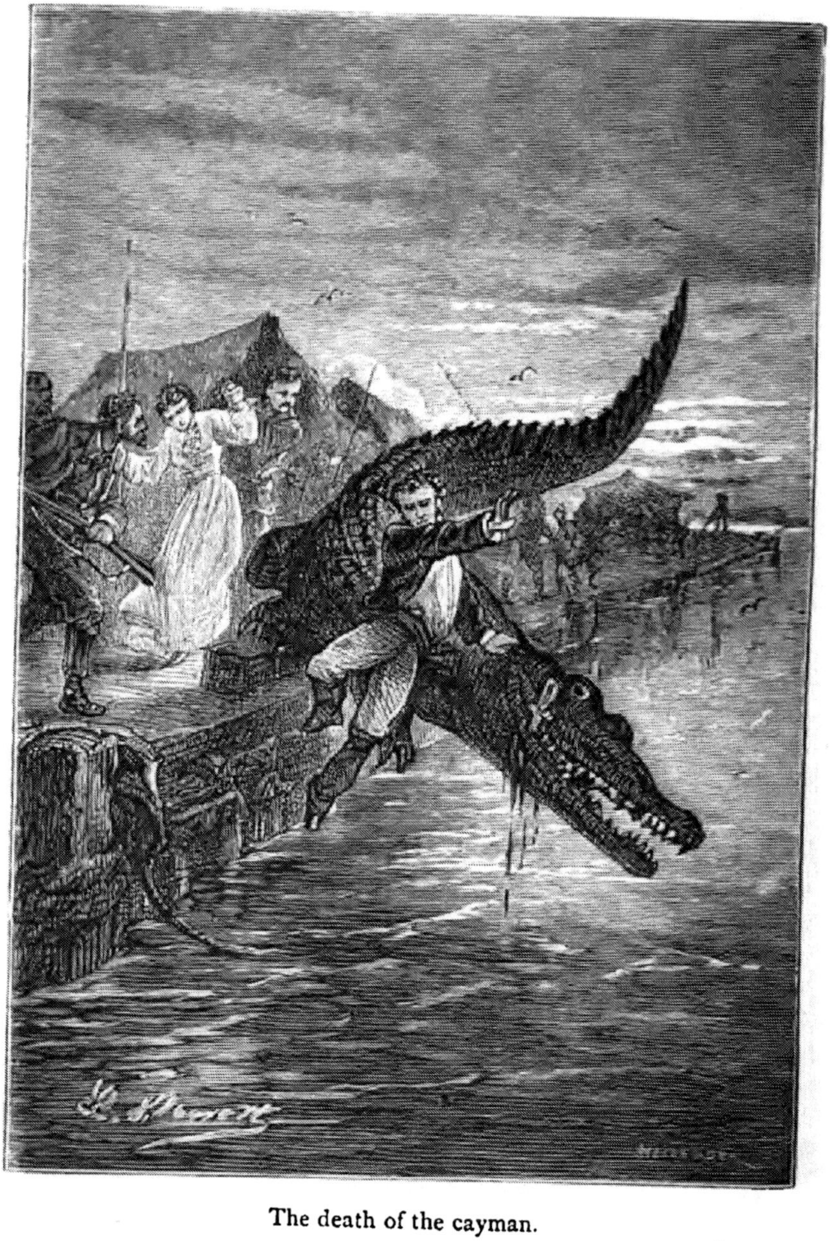

The death of the cayman.

Page 211.

having his arm snapped off by the two jaws, had they quickly closed.

Fragoso pulled out his arm in time, but he could not avoid the shock of the cayman, and was hurled back into the river, whose waters reddened all around.

"Fragoso! Fragoso!" shrieked Lina, kneeling on the edge of the raft.

A second afterwards Fragoso reappeared on the surface of the Amazon—safe and sound.

But, at the peril of his life he had saved the young girl, who soon came to. And as all hands were held out to him, Manoel's, Yaquita's, Minha's, and Lina's, and he did not know what to say, he ended by squeezing the hands of the young mulatto.

However, though Fragoso had saved Minha, it was assuredly to the intervention of Torres that Joam Garral owed his safety.

It was not, therefore, the fazender's life that the adventurer wanted. In the face of this fact, so much had to be admitted.

Manoel said this to Benito in an undertone.

"That is true!" replied Benito, embarrassed. "You are right, and in a sense it is one cruel care the less! Nevertheless, Manoel, my suspicions still exist! It is not always a man's worst enemy who wishes him dead!"

Joam Garral walked up to Torres.

"Thank you, Torres!" he said, holding out his hand. The adventurer took a step or two backwards without replying.

"Torres," continued Joam, "I am sorry that we are arriving at the end of our voyage, and that in a few days we must part! I owe you—"

"Joam Garral," answered Torres, "you owe me nothing! Your life is precious to me above all things! But if you will allow me—I have been thinking—in place of stopping at Manaos, I will go on to Belem. Will you take me there?"

Joam Garral replied by an affirmative nod.

In hearing this demand Benito in an unguarded moment was about to intervene, but Manoel stopped him, and the young man checked himself, though not without a violent effort.

CHAPTER XVIII.

THE ARRIVAL DINNER.

IN the morning, after a night which was scarcely sufficient to calm so much excitement, they unmoored from the cayman beach and departed. Before five days, if nothing interfered with their voyage, the raft would reach the port of Manaos.

Minha had quite recovered from her fright, and her eyes and smiles thanked all those who had risked their lives for her.

As for Lina, it seemed as though she was more grateful to the brave Fragoso than if it was herself that he had saved.

"I will pay you back, sooner or later, Mr. Fragoso!" said she, smiling.

"And how, Miss Lina?"

"Oh! You know very well!"

"Then if I know it, let it be soon and not late!" replied the good-natured fellow.

And from this day it began to be whispered about that the charming Lina was engaged to Fragoso, that their marriage would take place at the same time as that of Minha and Manoel, and that the young couple would remain at Belem with the others.

"Capital! capital!" repeated Fragoso, unceasingly; "but I never thought Para was such a long way off!"

As for Manoel and Benito, they had had a long conversation about what had passed. There could be no question about obtaining from Joam Garral the dismissal of his rescuer.

"Your life is precious to me above all things!" Torres had said.

This reply, hyperbolical and enigmatical at the time, Benito had heard and remembered.

In the meantime the young men could do nothing. More than ever they were reduced to waiting—to waiting not for four or five days, but for seven or eight weeks—that is to say, for whatever time it would take for the raft to get to Belem.

"There is in all this some mystery that I cannot understand," said Benito.

"Yes, but we are assured on one point," answered Manoel. "It is certain that Torres does not want your father's life. For the rest, we must still watch!"

It seemed that from this day Torres desired to keep

himself more reserved. He did not seek to intrude on the family, and was even less assiduous towards Minha. There seemed a relief in the situation of which all, save perhaps Joam Garral, felt the gravity.

On the evening of the same day they left on the right the island of Baroso, formed by a furo of that name, and Lake Manaori, which is fed by a confused series of petty tributaries.

The night passed without incident, though Joam Garral had advised them to watch with great care.

On the morrow, the 20th of August, the pilot, who kept near the right bank on account of the uncertain eddies on the left, entered between the bank and the islands.

Beyond this bank the country was dotted with large and small lakes, much as those of Calderon, Huarandeina, and other black-watered lagoons. This water-system marks the approach of the Rio Negro, the most remarkable of all the tributaries of the Amazon. In reality the main river still bore the name of the Solimoens, and it is only after the junction of the Rio Negro that it takes the name which has made it celebrated among the rivers of the globe.

During this day the raft had to be worked under curious conditions.

The arm followed by the pilot, between Calderon Island and the shore, was very narrow, although it appeared sufficiently large. This was owing to a great portion of the island being slightly below the mean level, but still covered by the high flood waters. On each side were massed forests of giant trees, whose summits towered some fifty feet above the ground, and joining one bank to the other formed an immense cradle.

On the left nothing could be more picturesque than this flooded forest, which seemed to have been planted in the middle of a lake. The stems of the trees arose from the clear, still water, in which every interlacement of their boughs was reflected with unequalled purity. They were arranged on an immense sheet of glass, like the trees in miniature on some table epergne, and their reflection could not be more perfect. The difference between the image and the reality could scarcely be described. Duplicates of grandeur, terminated above and below by a vast parasol of green, they seemed to form two hemispheres, inside which the jangada appeared to follow one of the great circles.

It had been necessary to bring the raft under these boughs, against which flowed the gentle current of the stream. It was impossible to go back. Hence the task of navigating with extreme care, so as to avoid the collisions on either side.

In this all Araujo's ability was shown, and he was admirably seconded by his crew. The trees of the forest furnished the resting-places for the long poles which kept

The road through the forest.

Page 216.

the jangada in its course. The least blow to the jangada
would have endangered the complete demolition of the
woodwork, and caused the loss, if not of the crew, of the
greater part of the cargo.

"It is truly very beautiful," said Minha, "and it would
be very pleasant for us always to travel in this way, on this
quiet water, shaded from the rays of the sun."

"At the same time pleasant and dangerous, dear Minha,"
said Manoel. "In a pirogue there is doubtless nothing to
fear in sailing here, but on a huge raft of wood better have
a free course and a clear stream.

"We shall be quite through the forest in a couple of
hours," said the pilot.

"Look well at it, then!" said Lina. "All these beautiful things pass so quickly! Ah! dear mistress! do you
see the troops of monkeys disporting in the higher
branches, and the birds admiring themselves in the pel-
lucid water!"

"And the flowers half-opened on the surface," replied
Minha, "and which the current dandles like the breeze!"

"And the long lianas, which so oddly stretch from one
tree to another!" added the young mulatto.

"And no Fragoso at the end of them!" said Lina's
betrothed. "That was rather a nice flower you gathered
in the forest of Iquitos!"

"Just behold the flower—the only one in the world,"

said Lina quizzingly; "and, mistress! just look at the splendid plants!"

And Lina pointed to the nymphæas with their colossal leaves, whose flowers bear buds as large as cocoa-nuts. Then, just where the banks plunged beneath the waters, there were clumps of "mucumus," reeds with large leaves, whose elastic stems bend to give passage to the pirogues and close again behind them. There was there what would tempt any sportsman, for a whole world of aquatic birds fluttered between the higher clusters, which shook with the stream.

Ibises half-lollingly posed on some old trunk, and grey herons motionless on one leg, solemn flamingoes who from a distance looked like red umbrellas scattered in the foliage, and phenicopters of every colour, enlivened the temporary morass.

And along the top of the water glided long and swiftly-swimming snakes, among them the formidable gymnotus, whose electric discharges successively repeated paralyze the most robust of men or animals, and end by dealing death. Precautions had to be taken against the "sucurijus" serpents, which, coiled round the trunk of some tree, unroll themselves, hang down, seize their prey, and draw it into their rings, which, are powerful enough to crush a bullock. Have there not been met with in these Amazonian forests reptiles from thirty to thirty-five feet long?

The river plants.

Page 218.

a jovial repast.   It was fitting to drink to the health of Amazones a few glasses of that generous liquor which comes
from the coasts of Oporto and Setubal.   Besides, this was,
in a way, the betrothal dinner of Fragoso and the charming Lina—that of Manoel and Minha had taken place at
the fazenda of Iquitos several weeks before.   After the
young master and mistress, it was the turn of the faithful
couple who were attached to them by so many bonds of
gratitude.

So Lina, who was to remain in the service of Minha,
and Fragoso, who was about to enter into that of Manoel
Valdez, sat at the common table, and even had the places
of honour reserved for them.

Torres naturally was present at the dinner, which was
worthy of the larder and kitchen of the jangada.

The adventurer seated opposite to Joam Garral, who was
always taciturn, listened to all that was said, but took no
part in the conversation.   Benito quietly and attentively
watched him.   The eyes of Torres, with a peculiar expression, constantly sought his father.   One would have called
them the eyes of some wild beast trying to fascinate his
prey before he sprang on it.

Manoel talked mostly with Minha.   Between whiles his
eyes wandered to Torres, but he acted his part more successfully than Benito in a situation which, if it did not finish
at Manaos, would certainly end at Belem.

The dinner was jolly enough, Lina kept it going with her good-humour, Fragoso with his witty repartees.

The Padre Passanha looked gaily round on the little world he cherished, and on the two young couples which his hands would shortly bless in the waters of Para.

"Eat, padre," said Benito, who joined in the general conversation ; " do honour to this betrothal dinner. You will want some strength to celebrate both marriages at once !"

"Well, my dear boy," replied Passanha, "seek out some lovely and gentle girl who wishes you well, and you will see that I can marry you at the same time !"

"Well answered, padre !" exclaimed Manoel. " Let us drink to the coming marriage of Benito."

"We must look out for some nice young lady at Belem," said Minha. " He should do what everybody else does."

" To the wedding of Mr. Benito !" said Fragoso, "who ought to wish all the world to marry him !"

"They are right, sir," said Yaquita. " I also drink to your marriage, and may you be as happy as Minha and Manoel, and as I and your father have been !"

" As you always will be, it is to be hoped," said Torres, drinking a glass of port without having pledged anybody. " All here have their happiness in their own hands."

It was difficult to say, but this wish, coming from the adventurer, left an unpleasant impression.

Manoel felt this, and wishing to destroy its effect, " Look

here, padre," said he, "while we are on this subject, are
there not any more couples to betroth on the raft?"

"I do not know," answered Padre Passanha, "unless
Torres—you are not married, I believe?"

"No; I am, and always shall be, a bachelor."

Benito and Manoel thought that while thus speaking
Torres looked towards Minha.

"And what should prevent you marrying?" replied
Padre Passanha; "at Belem you could find a wife whose
age would suit yours, and it would be possible perhaps for
you to settle in that town. That would be better than
this wandering life, of which, up to the present, you have
not made so very much."

"You are right, padre," answered Torres; "I do not say
no. Besides the example is contagious. Seeing all these
young couples gives me rather a longing for marriage.
But I am quite a stranger in Belem, and, for certain reasons,
that would make my settlement more difficult."

"Where do you come from, then?" asked Fragoso, who
always had the idea that he had already met Torres somewhere.

"From the province of Minas Geraes."

"And you were born—"

"In the capital of the diamond district, Tijuco."

Those who had seen Joam Garral at this moment would
have been surprised at the fixity of his look which met that
of Torres.

CHAPTER XIX.

ANCIENT HISTORY.

BUT the conversation was continued by Fragoso, who immediately rejoined,—

"What! you come from Tijuco, from the very capital of the diamond district?"

"Yes," said Torres. "Do you hail from that province?"

"No! I come from the Atlantic sea-board in the north of Brazil," replied Fragoso.

"You do not know this diamond country, Mr. Manoel?" asked Torres.

A negative shake of the head from the young man was the only reply.

"And you, Mr. Benito," continued Torres, addressing the younger Garral, whom he evidently wished to join in the conversation; "you have never had curiosity enough to visit the diamond arraval?"

"Never," drily replied Benito.

"Ah! I should like to see that country," said Fragoso, who unconsciously played Torres's game. "It seems to me I should finish by picking up a diamond worth something considerable."

"And what would you do with this diamond worth something considerable, Fragoso?" asked Lina.

"Sell it!"

"Then you would get rich all of a sudden!"

"Very rich!"

"Well, if you had been rich three months ago you would never have had the idea of—that liana?"

"And if I had not had that," exclaimed Fragoso, "I should not have found a charming little wife who—well, assuredly, all is for the best!"

"You see, Fragoso," said Minha, "when you marry Lina, diamond takes the place of diamond, and you do not lose by the change!"

"To be sure, Miss Minha," gallantly replied Fragoso; "rather I gain!"

There could be no doubt that Torres did not want the subject to drop, for he went on with,—

"It is a fact that at Tijuco sudden fortunes are realized enough to turn any man's head! Have you heard tell of the famous diamond of Abaete, which was valued at more than two million contos of reis? Well, this stone, which weighed an ounce, came from the Brazilian mines! And

they were three convicts—yes! three men sentenced to
transportation for life—who found it by chance in the
River Abaete, at ninety leagues from Terro de Frio."

"At a stroke their fortune was made?" asked Fragoso.

"No," replied Torres; "the diamond was handed over to
the governor-general of the mines. The value of the stone
was recognized, and King John VI., of Portugal, had it cut,
and wore it on his neck on great occasions. As for the
convicts, they got their pardon, but that was all, and the
cleverest could not get much of an income out of that!"

"You, doubtless?" said Benito very drily.

"Yes—I? Why not?" answered Torres. "Have you
ever been to the diamond district?" added he, this time
addressing Joam Garral.

"Never!" said Joam, looking straight at him.

"That is a pity!" replied he. "You should go there
one day. It is a very curious place, I assure you. The
diamond valley is an isolated spot in the vast empire of
Brazil, something like a park of a dozen leagues in circumference, which in the nature of its soil, its vegetation,
and its sandy rocks surrounded by a circle of high mountains, differs considerably from the neighbouring provinces.
But, as I have told you, it is one of the richest places in
the world, for from 1807 to 1817 the annual return was about
eighteen thousand carats. Ah! there have been some rare
finds there, not only for the climbers who seek the precious

Q

stone up to the very tops of the mountains, but also for the smugglers who fraudulently export it. But the work in the mines is not so pleasant, and the two thousand negroes employed in that work by the government are obliged even to divert the water-courses to get at the diamantiferous sand. Formerly it was easier work."

"In short," said Fragoso, "the good time has gone!"

" But what is still easy is to get the diamonds in scoundrel-fashion—that is, by theft ; and—stop! in 1826, when I was about eight years old, a terrible drama happened at Tijuco, which showed that criminals would recoil from nothing if they could gain a fortune by one bold stroke. But perhaps you are not interested ?"

" On the contrary, Torres ; go on," replied Joam Garral, in a singularly calm voice.

"So be it," answered Torres. "Well, the story is about stealing diamonds, and a handful of those pretty stones is worth a million, sometimes two!"

And Torres, whose face expressed the vilest sentiments of cupidity, almost unconsciously made a gesture of opening and shutting his hand.

"This is what happened," he continued. "At Tijuco it is customary to send off in one delivery the diamonds collected during the year. They are divided into two lots, according to their size, after being sorted in a dozen sieves with holes of different dimensions. These lots are put into

The brave defence.

Page 227.

sacks and forwarded to Rio de Janeiro ; but as they are worth many millions you may imagine they are heavily escorted. A workman chosen by the superintendent, four cavalrymen from the district regiment, and ten men on foot, complete the convoy. They first make for Villa Rica, where the commandant puts his seal on the sacks, and then the convoy continues its journey to Rio de Janeiro. I should add that, for the sake of precaution, the start is always kept secret. Well, in 1826, a young fellow named Dacosta, who was about twenty-two or twenty-three years of age, and who for some years had been employed at Tijuco in the offices of the governor-general, devised the following scheme. He leagued himself with a band of smugglers, and informed them of the date of the departure of the convoy. The scoundrels took their measures accordingly. They were numerous and well armed. Close to Villa Rica, during the night of the 22nd January, the gang suddenly attacked the diamond escort, who defended themselves bravely, but were all massacred, with the exception of one man, who, seriously wounded, managed to escape, and bring the news of the horrible deed. The workman was not spared any more than the soldiers. He fell beneath the blows of the thieves, and was doubtless dragged away and thrown over some precipice, for his body was never found."

"And this Dacosta ?" asked Joam Garral.

"Well, his crime did not do him much good, for suspicion soon pointed towards him.   He was accused of having got up the affair.   In vain he protested that he was innocent. Thanks to the situation he held, he was in a position to know the date on which the convoy's departure was to take place.   He alone could have informed the smugglers. He was charged, arrested, tried, and sentenced to death. Such a sentence required his execution in twenty-four hours."

"Was the fellow executed?" asked Fragoso.

"No," replied Torres; "they shut him up in the prison at Villa Rica, and during the night, a few hours only before his execution, whether alone or helped by others, he managed to escape."

"Has this young man been heard of since?" asked Joam Garral.

"Never," replied Torres.   "He probably left Brazil, and now, in some distant land, lives a cheerful life with the proceeds of the robbery which he is sure to have realized."

"Perhaps, on the other hand, he died miserably!" answered Joam Garral.

"And, perhaps," added Padre Passanha, "Heaven caused him to feel remorse for his crime."

Here they all rose from the table, and having finished their dinner, went out to breathe the evening air.   The sun was low on the horizon, but an hour had still to elapse before nightfall.

"These stories are not very lively," said Fragoso; "and our betrothal dinner was best at the beginning?"

"But it was your fault, Fragoso," answered Lina.

"How my fault?"

"It was you who went on talking about the district and the diamonds, when you should not have done so."

"Well, that's true," replied Fragoso; "but I had no idea we were going to wind up in that fashion."

"You are the first to blame!"

"And the first to be punished, Miss Lina; for I did not hear you laugh all through the dessert."

The whole family strolled towards the bow of the jangada. Manoel and Benito walked one behind the other without speaking. Yaquita and her daughter silently followed, and all felt an unaccountable impression of sadness, as if they had a presentiment of some coming calamity.

Torres stepped up to Joam Garral, who, with bowed head, seemed to be lost in thought, and putting his hand on his shoulder, said, "Joam Garral, may I have a few minutes' conversation with you?"

Joam looked at Torres.

"Here?" he asked.

"No; in private."

"Come, then."

They went towards the house, entered it, and the door was shut on them.

It would be difficult to depict what every one felt when Joam Garral and Torres disappeared. What could there be in common between the adventurer and the honest fazender of Iquitos? The menace of some frightful misfortune seemed to hang over the whole family, and they scarcely dared speak to each other.

"Manoel!" said Benito, seizing his friend's arm, "whatever happens, this man must leave us to-morrow at Manaos."

"Yes! it is imperative!" answered Manoel.

"And if through him some misfortune happens to my father—I shall kill him!"

CHAPTER XX.

BETWEEN THE TWO MEN.

FOR a moment, alone in the room, where none could see or hear them, Joam Garral and Torres looked at each other without uttering a word. Did the adventurer hesitate to speak? Did he suspect that Joam Garral would only reply to his demands by a scornful silence?

Yes! Probably so. So Torres did not question him. At the outset of the conversation he took the affirmative, and assumed the part of an accuser.

"Joam," he said, "your name is not Garral. Your name is Dacosta!"

At the guilty name which Torres thus gave him, Joam Garral could not repress a slight shudder.

"You are Joam Dacosta," continued Torres, "who, five-and-twenty years ago, were a clerk in the governor-general's office at Tijuco, and you are the man who was sentenced to death in this affair of the robbery and murder!"

No response from Joam Garral, whose strange tranquillity surprised the adventurer. Had he made a mistake in accusing his host? No! For Joam Garral made no start at the terrible accusations. Doubtless he wanted to know to what Torres was coming.

"Joam Dacosta, I repeat! It was you whom they sought for in this diamond affair, whom they convicted of crime and condemned to death, and it was you who escaped from the prison at Villa Rica a few hours before you should have been executed! Do you not answer?"

Rather a long silence followed this direct question which Torres asked. Joam Garral, still calm, took a seat. His elbow rested on a small table, and he looked fixedly at his accuser without bending his head.

"Will you reply?" repeated Torres.

"What reply do you want from me?" said Joam quietly.

"A reply," slowly answered Torres, "that will keep me from finding out the chief of the police at Manaos, and saying to him, 'A man is there whose identity can be easily established, who can be recognized even after twenty-five years' absence, and this man was the instigator of the diamond robbery at Tijuco. He was the accomplice of the murderers of the soldiers of the escort; he is the man who escaped from execution; he is Joam Garral, whose true name is Joam Dacosta.'"

"And so, Torres," said Joam Garral, "I shall have nothing to fear from you if I give the answer you require?"

"Nothing, for then neither you nor I will have any interest in talking about the matter."

"Neither you nor I?" asked Joam Garral. "It is not with money, then, that your silence is to be bought?"

"No! No matter how much you offered me!"

"What do you want, then?"

"Joam Garral," replied Torres, "here is my proposal. Do not be in a hurry to reply by a formal refusal. Remember that you are in my power."

"What is this proposal?" asked Joam.

Torres hesitated for a moment.

The attitude of this guilty man, whose life he held in his hands, was enough to astonish him. He had expected a stormy discussion and prayers and tears. He had before him a man convicted of the most heinous of crimes, and the man never flinched.

At length, crossing his arms, he said,—

"You have a daughter!—I like her,—and I want to marry her!"

Apparently Joam Garral expected anything from such a man, and was as quiet as before.

"And so," he said, "the worthy Torres is anxious to enter the family of a murderer and a thief?"

"I am the sole judge of what it suits me to do," said Torres. "I wish to be the son-in-law of Joam Garral, and I will."

"You ignore, then, that my daughter is going to marry Manoel Valdez!"

"You will break it off with Manoel Valdez!"

"And if my daughter declines?"

"If you tell her all, I have no doubt she would consent," was the impudent answer.

"All?"

"All, if necessary. Between her own feelings and the honour of her family and the life of her father she would not hesitate."

"You are a consummate scoundrel, Torres," quietly said Joam, whose coolness never forsook him.

"A scoundrel and a murderer were made to understand each other."

At these words Joam Garral rose, advanced to the adventurer, and looking him straight in the face, "Torres," he said, "if you wish to become one of the family of Joam Dacosta, you ought to know that Joam Dacosta was innocent of the crime for which he was condemned."

"Really!"

"And I add," replied Joam, "that you hold the proof of his innocence, and are keeping it back to proclaim it on the day when you marry his daughter."

"Fair play, Joam Garral," answered Torres, lowering his voice, "and when you have heard me out, you will see if you dare refuse me your daughter!"

"I am listening, Torres."

"Well," said the adventurer, half keeping back his words, as if he was sorry to let them escape from his lips, "I know you are innocent! I know it, for I know the true culprit, and I am in a position to prove your innocence."

"And the unhappy man who committed the crime?"

"Is dead."

"Dead!" exclaimed Joam Garral; and the word made him turn pale, in spite of himself, as if it had deprived him of all power of reinstatement.

"Dead," repeated Torres; "but this man, whom I knew a long time after his crime, and without knowing that he was a convict, had written out at length, in his own hand, the story of this affair of the diamonds, even to the smallest details. Feeling his end approaching, he was seized with remorse. He knew where Joam Dacosta had taken refuge, and under what name the innocent man had again begun a new life. He knew that he was rich, in the bosom of a happy family, but he knew also that there was no happiness for him. And this happiness he desired to add to the reputation to which he was entitled. But death came—he entrusted to me, his companion, to do what he could no longer do. He gave me the proofs of Dacosta's innocence for me to transmit to him, and he died."

"The man's name?" exclaimed Joam Garral, in a tone he could not control.

"You will know it when I am one of your family."

"And the writing?"

Joam Garral was ready to throw himself on Torres, to search him, to snatch from him the proofs of his innocence.

"The writing is in a safe place," replied Torres, "and you will not have it until your daughter has become my wife. Now will you still refuse me?"

"Yes," replied Joam, "but in return for that paper the half of my fortune is yours."

"The half of your fortune!" exclaimed Torres; "agreed, on condition that Minha brings it to me at her marriage."

"And it is thus that you respect the wishes of a dying man, of a criminal tortured by remorse, and who has charged you to repair as much as he could the evil which he had done?"

"It is thus."

"Once more, Torres," said Joam Garral, "you are a consummate scoundrel."

"Be it so."

"And as I am not a criminal we were not made to understand one another."

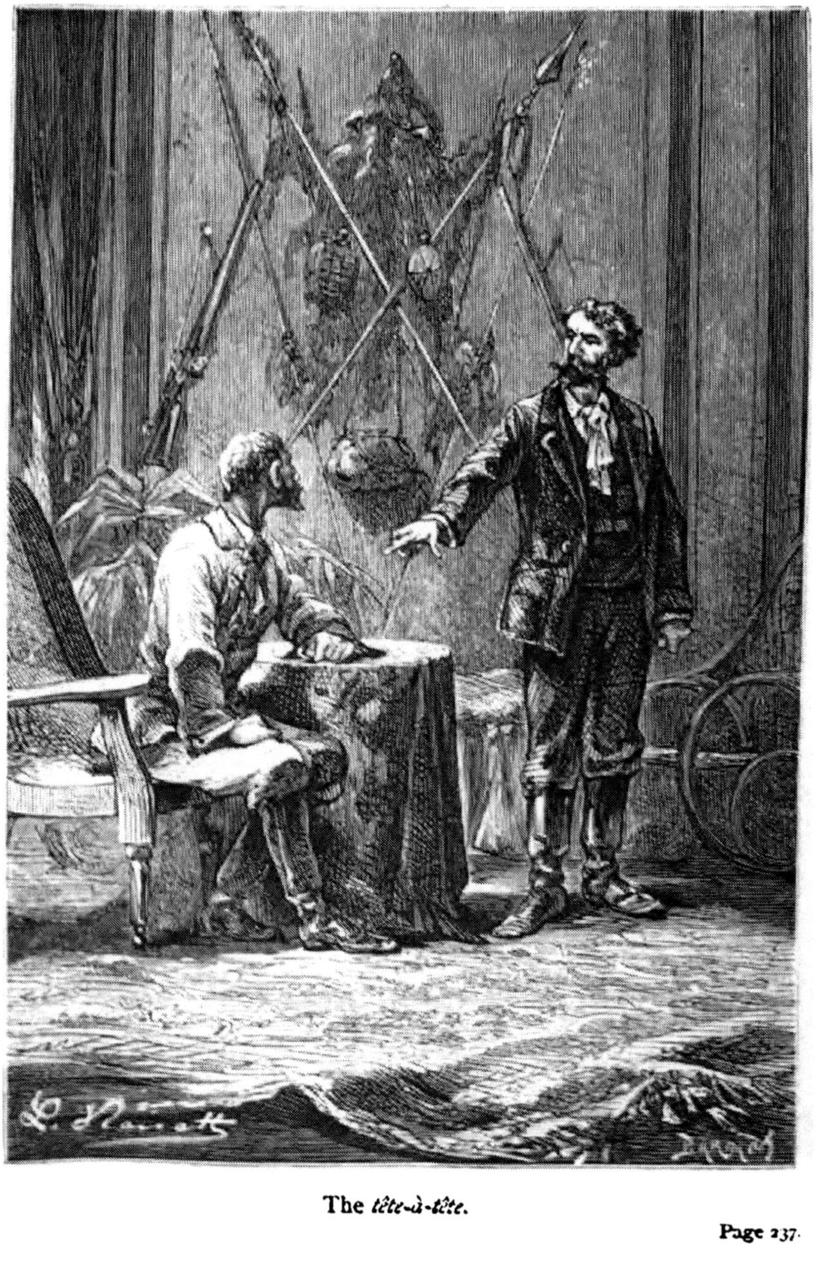

The *tête-à-tête.*

Page 237.

" And you refuse ? "

" I refuse."

" It will be your ruin, then, Joam Garral. Everything accuses you in the proceedings that have already taken place. You are condemned to death, and you know, in sentences for crimes of that nature, the government is forbidden the right of commuting the penalty. Denounced, you are taken ; taken, you are executed. And I will denounce you."

Master as he was of himself, Joam could stand it no longer. He was about to rush on Torres.

A gesture from the rascal cooled his anger.

" Take care," said Torres, " your wife knows not that she is the wife of Joam Dacosta, your children do not know they are the children of Joam Dacosta, and you are going to give them the information."

Joam Garral stopped himself. He regained his usual command over himself, and his features recovered their habitual calm.

" This discussion has lasted long enough," said he, moving towards the door, " and I know what there is left for me to do."

" Take care, Joam Garral ! " said Torres, for the last time, for he could scarcely believe that his ignoble attempt at extortion had collapsed.

Joam Garral made him no answer. He threw back the

door which opened under the verandah, made a sign to
Torres to follow him, and they advanced towards the
centre of the jangada, where the family were assem-
bled.

Benito, Manoel, and all of them, under a feeling of deep
anxiety, had risen. They could see that the bearing of
Torres was still menacing, and that the fire of anger still
shone in his eyes.

In extraordinary contrast, Joam Garral was master of
himself, and almost smiling.

Both of them stopped before Yaquita and her people.
Not one dared to say a word to them.

It was Torres who, in a hollow voice, and with his customary impudence, broke the painful silence.

"For the last time, Joam Garral," he said, "I ask you
for a last reply!"

"And here is my reply."

And addressing his wife,—

"Yaquita," he said, "peculiar circumstances oblige me
to alter what we have formerly decided as to the marriage
of Minha and Manoel."

"At last!" exclaimed Torres.

Joam Garral, without answering him, shot at the adventurer a glance of the deepest scorn.

But at the words, Manoel had felt his heart beat as if it
would break. The girl arose, ashy pale, as if she would

seek shelter by the side of her mother. Yaquita opened her arms to protect, to defend her.

"Father!" said Benito, who had placed himself between Joam Garral and Torres, "what were you going to say?"

"I was going to say," answered Joam Garral, raising his voice, "that to wait for our arrival in Para for the wedding of Minha and Manoel is to wait too long! The marriage will take place here, not later than to-morrow, on the jangada, with the aid of Padre Passanha, if, after a conversation I am about to have with Manoel, he agrees with me to defer it no longer."

"Ah, father! father!" exclaimed the young man.

"Wait a little before you call me so, Manoel!" replied Joam, in a tone of unspeakable suffering.

Here Torres, with crossed arms, gave the whole family a look of inconceivable insolence.

"So that is your last word?" said he, extending his hand towards Joam Garral.

"No, that is not my last word."

"What is it, then?"

"This, Torres! I am master here! You will be off, if you please, and even if you do not please, and leave the jangada this very instant!"

"Yes, this instant!" exclaimed Benito; "or I will throw you overboard."

Torres shrugged his shoulders.

"No threats," he said ; "they are of no use!   It suits me also to land, and without delay.   But you will remember me, Joam Garral.   We shall not be long before we meet."

"If it only depends on me," answered Joam Garral, "we shall soon meet, and rather sooner, perhaps, than you will like.   To-morrow I shall be with Judge Ribeiro, the first magistrate of the province, whom I have advised of my arrival at Manaos.   If you dare, meet me there ! "

"At Judge Ribeiro's ? " said Torres, evidently discon-certed.

"At Judge Ribeiro's," answered Joam Garral.

And then, showing the pirogue to Torres, with a gesture of supreme contempt, Joam Garral ordered four of his people to land him without delay on the nearest point of the island.

The scoundrel at last disappeared.

The family, who were still appalled, respected the silence of its chief ; but Fragoso, comprehending scarce half the gravity of the situation, and carried away by his customary vivacity, came up to Joam Garral.

"If the wedding of Miss Minha and Mr. Manoel is to take place to-morrow on the raft—"

"Yours shall take place at the same time," kindly an-swered Joam Garral.

And making a sign to Manoel, he retired to his room with him.

The interview between Joam and Manoel had lasted for half an hour, and it seemed a century to the family, when the door of the room was reopened.

Manoel came out alone ; his face glowed with generous resolution.

Going up to Yaquita, he said, " My mother ! " to Minha he said, " My wife ! " to Benito he said, " My brother ! " and, turning towards Lina and Fragoso, he said to all, " To-morrow ! "

He knew all that had passed between Joam Garral and Torres. He knew that, counting on the protection of Judge Ribeiro, by means of a correspondence which he had had with him for a year past without speaking of it to his people, Joam Garral had at last succeeded in clearing himself and convincing him of his innocence. He knew that Joam Garral had boldly undertaken the voyage with the sole object of cancelling the hateful proceedings of which he had been the victim, so as not to leave on his daughter and son-in-law the weight of the terrible situation which he had had to endure so long himself.

Yes, Manoel knew all this, and, further, he knew that Joam Garral—or rather Joam Dacosta—was innocent, and his misfortunes made him even dearer and more devoted to him. What he did not know was that the material proof of the innocence of the fazender existed, and that this proof was in the hands of Torres. Joam Garral wished

R

to reserve for the judge himself the use of this proof, which, if the adventurer had spoken truly, would demonstrate his innocence.

Manoel confined himself, then, to announcing that he was going to Padre Passanha to ask him to get things ready for the two weddings.

Next day, the 24th of August, scarcely an hour before the ceremony was to take place, a large pirogue came off from the left bank of the river and hailed the jangada. A dozen paddlers had swiftly brought it from Manaos, and with a few men it carried the chief of the police, who made himself known and came on board.

At the moment Joam Garral and his family, attired for the ceremony, were coming out of the house.

"Joam Garral?" asked the chief of the police.

"I am here," replied Joam.

"Joam Garral," continued the chief of the police, "you have also been Joam Dacosta; both names have been borne by the same man—I arrest you!"

At these words Yaquita and Minha, struck with stupor, stopped, without any power to move.

"My father a murderer?" exclaimed Benito, rushing towards Joam Garral.

By a gesture his father silenced him.

"I will only ask you one question," said Joam, with firm voice, addressing the chief of police. "Has the warrant in

Joam's arrest.

Page 243.

virtue of which you arrest me been issued against me by the justice at Manaos—by Judge Ribeiro?"

" No," answered the chief of the police, " it was given to me, with an order for its immediate execution, by his substitute. Judge Ribeiro was struck with apoplexy yesterday evening, and died during the night at two o'clock, without having recovered his consciousness."

" Dead!" exclaimed Joam Garral, crushed for a moment by the news—" dead! dead!"

But soon raising his head, he said to his wife and children, "Judge Ribeiro alone knew that I was innocent, my dear ones. The death of the judge may be fatal to me, but that is no reason for me to despair."

And, turning towards Manoel, "Heaven help us!" he said to him; " we shall see if truth will come down to the earth from Above."

The chief of the police made a sign to his men, who advanced to secure Joam Garral.

" But speak, father!" shouted Benito, mad with despair; " say one word, and we shall contest even by force this horrible mistake of which you are the victim!"

" There is no mistake here, my son," replied Joam Garral; " Joam Dacosta and Joam Garral are one. I am in truth Joam Dacosta! I am the honest man whom a legal error unjustly doomed to death five-and-twenty years ago in the place of the true culprit! That I am quite innocent I swear before Heaven, once for all, on your heads, my children, and on the head of your mother !"

"All communication between you and yours is now forbidden," said the chief of the police. "You are my prisoner, Joam Garral, and I will rigorously execute my warrant."

Joam restrained by a gesture his dismayed children and servants.

"Let the justice of man be done while we wait for the justice of God !"

And with his head unbent, he stepped into the pirogue.

It seemed, indeed, as though of all present Joam Garral was the only one whom this fearful thunderbolt, which had fallen so unexpectedly on his head, had failed to overwhelm.

THE END OF THE FIRST PART.

PRINTED BY GILBERT AND RIVINGTON, LIMITED, ST. JOHN'S SQUARE, LONDON.

A Catalogue of American and Foreign Books Published or Imported by MESSRS. SAMPSON LOW & CO. *can be had on application.*

Crown Buildings, 188, *Fleet Street, London,*
January, 1881.

𝔄 𝔖election from t𝔥e 𝔏ist of 𝔅ooks

PUBLISHED BY

SAMPSON LOW, MARSTON, SEARLE, & RIVINGTON.

ALPHABETICAL LIST.

A CLASSIFIED Educational Catalogue of Works published in Great Britain. Demy 8vo, cloth extra. Second Edition, revised and corrected to Christmas, 1879, 5*s*

About Some Fellows. By an ETON BOY, Author of "A Day of my Life." Cloth limp, square 16n₁o, 2*s*. 6*d*.

Adventures of Captain Mago. A Phœnician's Explorations 1000 years B.C. By LEON CAHUN. Numerous Illustrations. Crown 8vo, cloth extra, gilt edges, 7*s*. 6*d*. ; plainer binding, 5*s*.

Adventures of a Young Naturalist. By LUCIEN BIART, with 117 beautiful Illustrations on Wood. Edited and adapted by PARKER GILLMORE. Post 8vo, cloth extra, gilt edges, New Edition, 7*s*. 6*d*.

Afghan Knife (The). A Novel. By ROBERT ARMITAGE STERNDALE, Author of "Seonee." Small post 8vo, cloth extra, 6*s*.

After Sundown ; or, The Palette and the Pen. By W. W. FENN, Author of "Blind-Man's Holiday," &c. With Portrait of Author. 2 vols., crown 8vo, cloth extra, 24*s*.

Albania : A Narrative of Recent Travel. By E. F. KNIGHT. With some very good Illustrations specially made for the work. Crown 8vo, cloth extra, 12*s*. 6*d*.

Alcott (Louisa M.) *Jimmy's Cruise in the "Pinafore."* With 9 Illustrations. Second Edition. Small post 8vo, cloth gilt, 3*s*. 6*d*.

———— *Aunt Jo's Scrap-Bag.* Square 16mo, 2*s*. 6*d*. (Rose Library, 1*s*.)

———— *Little Men : Life at Plumfield with Jo's Boys.* Small post 8vo, cloth, gilt edges, 3*s*. 6*d*. (Rose Library, Double vol. 2*s*.)

———— *Little Women.* 1 vol., cloth, gilt edges, 3*s*. 6*d*. (Rose Library, 2 vols., 1*s*. each.)

A

Alcott (Louisa M.) Old-Fashioned Girl. Best Edition, small post 8vo, cloth extra, gilt edges, 3s. 6d. (Rose Library, 2s.)

——— *Work and Beginning Again.* A Story of Experience. 1 vol., small post 8vo, cloth extra, 6s. Several Illustrations. (Rose Library, 2 vols., 1s. each.)

——— *Shawl Straps.* Small post 8vo, cloth extra, gilt, 3s. 6d.

——— *Eight Cousins; or, the Aunt Hill.* Small post 8vo, with Illustrations, 3s. 6d.

——— *The Rose in Bloom.* Small post 8vo, cloth extra, 3s. 6d.

——— *Silver Pitchers.* Small post 8vo, cloth extra, 3s. 6d.

——— *Under the Lilacs.* Small post 8vo, cloth extra, 5s.

——— *Jack and Jill.* Small post 8vo, cloth extra, 5s.
"Miss Alcott's stories are thoroughly healthy, full of racy fun and humour . . . exceedingly entertaining . . . . We can recommend the 'Eight Cousins.'"—*Athenæum.*

Alpine Ascents and Adventures; or, Rock and Snow Sketches. By H. Schütz Wilson, of the Alpine Club. With Illustrations by Whymper and Marcus Stone. Crown 8vo, 10s. 6d. 2nd Edition.

Andersen (Hans Christian) Fairy Tales. With Illustrations in Colours by E. V. B. Royal 4to, cloth, 25s.

Architecture (The Twenty Styles of). By Dr. W. Wood, Author of "The Hundred Greatest Men." Imperial 8vo, with 52 Plates.

Art Education. See "Illustrated Text Books."

Autobiography of Sir G. Gilbert Scott, R.A., F.S.A., &c. Edited by his Son, G. Gilbert Scott. With an Introduction by the Dean of Chichester, and a Funeral Sermon, preached in Westminster Abbey, by the Dean of Westminster. Also, Portrait on steel from the portrait of the Author by G. Richmond, R.A. 1 vol., demy 8vo, cloth extra, 18s.

THE BAYARD SERIES,
Edited by the late J. Hain Friswell.
Comprising Pleasure Books of Literature produced in the Choicest Style as Companionable Volumes at Home and Abroad.
"We can hardly imagine better books for boys to read or for men to ponder over."—*Times.*
Price 2s. 6d. each Volume, complete in itself, flexible cloth extra, gilt edges, with silk Headbands and Registers.

The Story of the Chevalier Bayard. By M. De Berville.

De Joinville's St. Louis, King of France.

The Essays of Abraham Cowley, including all his Prose Works.

Abdallah; or, The Four Leaves. By Edouard Laboullaye.

The Bayard Series (continued) :—

Table-Talk and Opinions of Napoleon Buonaparte.

Vathek : An Oriental Romance. By William Beckford.

The King and the Commons. A Selection of Cavalier and Puritan Songs. Edited by Professor Morley.

Words of Wellington : Maxims and Opinions of the Great Duke.

Dr. Johnson's Rasselas, Prince of Abyssinia. With Notes.

Hazlitt's Round Table. With Biographical Introduction.

The Religio Medici, Hydriotaphia, and the Letter to a Friend. By Sir Thomas Browne, Knt.

Ballad Poetry of the Affections. By Robert Buchanan.

Coleridge's Christabel, and other

Imaginative Poems. With Preface by Algernon C. Swinburne.

Lord Chesterfield's Letters, Sentences, and Maxims. With Introduction by the Editor, and Essay on Chesterfield by M. de Ste.-Beuve, of the French Academy.

Essays in Mosaic. By Thos. Ballantyne.

My Uncle Toby ; his Story and his Friends. Edited by P. Fitzgerald.

Reflections ; or, Moral Sentences and Maxims of the Duke de la Rochefoucald.

Socrates : Memoirs for English Readers from Xenophon's Memorabilia. By Edw. Levien.

Prince Albert's Golden Precepts.

A Case containing 12 Volumes, price 31s. 6d.; or the Case separately, price 3s. 6d.

Beauty and the Beast. An Old Tale retold, with Pictures by E. V. B. 4to, cloth extra. 10 Illustrations in Colours. 12s. 6d.

Begum's Fortune (The) : A New Story. By JULES VERNE. Translated by W. H. G. KINGSTON. Numerous Illustrations. Crown 8vo, cloth, gilt edges, 7s. 6d. ; plainer binding, plain edges, 5s.

Ben Hur : A Tale of the Christ. By L. WALLACE. Crown 8vo, 6s.

Beumers' German Copybooks. In six gradations at 4d. each.

Biart (Lucien). See "Adventures of a Young Naturalist," "My Rambles in the New World," "The Two Friends," "Involuntary Voyage."

Bickersteth's Hymnal Companion to Book of Common Prayer may be had in various styles and bindings from 1d. to 21s. *Price List and Prospectus will be forwarded on application.*

Bickersteth (Rev. E. H., M.A.) The Reef, and other Parables. 1 vol., square 8vo, with numerous very beautiful Engravings, 2s. 6d.

—— *The Clergyman in his Home.* Small post 8vo, 1s.

—— *The Master's Home-Call; or, Brief Memorials of* Alice Frances Bickersteth. 20th Thousand. 32mo, cloth gilt, 1s.

—— *The Master's Will.* A Funeral Sermon preached on the Death of Mrs. S. Gurney Buxton. Sewn, 6d. ; cloth gilt, 1s.

Bickersteth (Rev. E. H., M.A.) The Shadow of the Rock. A Selection of Religious Poetry. 18mo, cloth extra, 2s. 6d.

——— *The Shadowed Home and the Light Beyond.* 7th Edition, crown 8vo, cloth extra, 5s.

Biographies of the Great Artists (Illustrated). Each of the following Volumes is illustrated with from twelve to twenty full-page Engravings, printed in the best manner, and bound in ornamental cloth cover, 3s. 6d. Library Edition, bound in a superior style, and handsomely ornamented, with gilt top; six Volumes, enclosed in a cloth case, with lid, £1 11s. 6d. each case.

Hogarth.	Fra Bartolommeo.	Sir David Wilkie.
Turner.	Giotto.	Van Eyck.
Rubens.	Raphael.	Figure Painters of
Holbein.	Van Dyck and Hals.	Holland.
Tintoretto.	Titian.	Michel Angelo.
Little Masters of	Rembrandt.	Delaroche and Vernet.
Germany.	Leonardo da Vinci.	Landseer.
Fra Angelico and	Gainsborough and	Reynolds.
Masaccio.	Constable.	

" Few things in the way of small books upon great subjects, avowedly cheap and necessarily brief, have been hitherto so well done as these biographies of the Great Masters in painting."—*Times.*

" A deserving series."—*Edinburgh Review.*

" Most thoroughly and tastefully edited."—*Spectator.*

Black (Wm.) Three Feathers. Small post 8vo, cloth extra, 6s.

——— *Lady Silverdale's Sweetheart, and other Stories.* 1 vol., small post 8vo, 6s.

——— *Kilmeny: a Novel.* Small post 8vo, cloth, 6s.

——— *In Silk Attire.* 3rd Edition, small post 8vo, 6s.

——— *A Daughter of Heth.* 11th Edition, small post 8vo, 6s.

——— *Sunrise.* 15 Monthly Parts, 1s. each.

Blackmore (R. D.) Lorna Doone. 10th Edition, cr. 8vo, 6s.

——— *Alice Lorraine.* 1 vol., small post 8vo, 6th Edition, 6s.

——— *Clara Vaughan.* Revised Edition, 6s.

——— *Cradock Nowell.* New Edition, 6s.

——— *Cripps the Carrier.* 3rd Edition, small post 8vo, 6s.

——— *Mary Anerley.* New Edition, 6s.

——— *Erema ; or, My Father's Sin.* With 12 Illustrations, small post 8vo, 6s.

Blossoms from the King's Garden : Sermons for Children. By the Rev. C. BOSANQUET. 2nd Edition, small post 8vo, cloth extra, 6s.

Blue Banner (The); or, The Adventures of a Mussulman, a Christian, and a Pagan, in the time of the Crusades and Mongol Conquest. Translated from the French of LEON CAHUN. With Seventy-six Wood Engravings. Imperial 16mo, cloth, gilt edges, 7s. 6d.; plainer binding, 5s.

Boy's Froissart (The). 7s. 6d. *See* " Froissart."

Boy's King Arthur (The). With very fine Illustrations. Square crown 8vo, cloth extra, gilt edges, 7s. 6d. Edited by SIDNEY LANIER, Editor of " The Boy's Froissart."

Brazil: the Amazons, and the Coast. By HERBERT H. SMITH. With 115 Full-page and other Illustrations. Demy 8vo, 650 pp., 21s.

Brazil and the Brazilians. By J. C. FLETCHER and D. P. KIDDER. 9th Edition, Illustrated, 8vo, 21s.

Breton Folk: An Artistic Tour in Brittany. By HENRY BLACKBURN, Author of " Artists and Arabs," " Normandy Picturesque," &c. With 171 Illustrations by RANDOLPH CALDECOTT. Imperial 8vo, cloth extra, gilt edges, 21s.

Bricks without Straw. By the Author of " A Fool's Errand." Crown 8vo, with numerous Illustrations, 7s. 6d.

British Goblins: Welsh Folk-Lore, Fairy Mythology, Legends, and Traditions. By WIRT SYKES, United States Consul for Wales. With Illustrations by J. H. THOMAS. This account of the Fairy Mythology and Folk-Lore of his Principality is, by permission, dedicated to H.R.H. the Prince of Wales. Second Edition. 8vo, 18s.

Buckle (Henry Thomas) The Life and Writings of. By ALFRED HENRY HUTH. With Portrait. 2 vols., demy 8vo.

Burnaby (Capt.) See " On Horseback."

Burnham Beeches (Heath, F. G.). With numerous Illustrations and a Map. Crown 8vo, cloth, gilt edges, 3s. 6d. Second Edition.

Butler (W. F.) The Great Lone Land; an Account of the Red River Expedition, 1869-70. With Illustrations and Map. Fifth and Cheaper Edition, crown 8vo, cloth extra, 7s. 6d.

———— *The Wild North Land; the Story of a Winter Journey* with Dogs across Northern North America. Demy 8vo, cloth, with numerous Woodcuts and a Map, 4th Edition, 18s. Cr. 8vo, 7s. 6d.

———— *Akim-foo: the History of a Failure.* Demy 8vo, cloth, 2nd Edition, 16s. Also, in crown 8vo, 7s. 6d.

CADOGAN (Lady A.) Illustrated Games of Patience. Twenty-four Diagrams in Colours, with Descriptive Text. Foolscap 4to, cloth extra, gilt edges, 3rd Edition, 12s. 6d.

Caldecott (R.). See " Breton Folk."

Celebrated Travels and Travellers. See VÉRNE.

Changed Cross (The), and other Religious Poems. 16mo, 2s. 6d.

Child of the Cavern (The); or, Strange Doings Underground. By JULES VERNE. Translated by W. H. G. KINGSTON. Numerous Illustrations. Sq. cr. 8vo, gilt edges, 7s. 6d.; cl., plain edges, 5s.

Child's Play, with 16 Coloured Drawings by E. V. B. Printed on thick paper, with tints, 7s. 6d.

——— *New.* By E. V. B. Similar to the above. *See* New.

——— A New and Cheap Edition of the two above; containing 48 Illustrations by E. V. B., printed in tint, handsomely bound, 3s. 6d.

Children's Lives and How to Preserve Them; or, The Nursery Handbook. By W. LOMAS, M.D. Crown 8vo, cloth, 5s.

Choice Editions of Choice Books. 2s. 6d. each, Illustrated by C. W. COPE, R.A., T. CRESWICK, R.A., E. DUNCAN, BIRKET FOSTER, J. C. HORSLEY, A.R.A., G. HICKS, R. REDGRAVE, R.A., C. STONEHOUSE, F. TAYLER, G. THOMAS, H. J. TOWNSHEND, E. H. WEHNERT, HARRISON WEIR, &c.

Bloomfield's Farmer's Boy.	Milton's L'Allegro.
Campbell's Pleasures of Hope.	Poetry of Nature. Harrison Weir.
Coleridge's Ancient Mariner.	Rogers' (Sam.) Pleasures of Memory.
Goldsmith's Deserted Village.	Shakespeare's Songs and Sonnets.
Goldsmith's Vicar of Wakefield.	Tennyson's May Queen.
Gray's Elegy in a Churchyard.	Elizabethan Poets.
Keat's Eve of St. Agnes.	Wordsworth's Pastoral Poems.

" Such works are a glorious beatification for a poet."—*Athenæum*.

Christ in Song. By Dr. PHILIP SCHAFF. A New Edition, Revised, cloth, gilt edges, 6s.

Cobbett (William). A Biography. By EDWARD SMITH. 2 vols., crown 8vo, 25s.

Confessions of a Frivolous Girl (The): A Novel of Fashionable Life. Edited by ROBERT GRANT. Crown 8vo, 6s.

Cradle-Land of Arts and Creeds; or, Nothing New under the Sun. By CHARLES J. STONE, Barrister-at-law, and late Advocate, High Courts, Bombay. 8vo, pp. 420, cloth, 14s.

Cripps the Carrier. 3rd Edition, 6s. *See* BLACKMORE.

Cruise of H.M.S. " Challenger" (The). By W. J. J. SPRY, R.N. With Route Map and many Illustrations. 6th Edition, demy 8vo, cloth, 18s. Cheap Edition, crown 8vo, some of the Illustrations, 7s. 6d.

Curious Adventures of a Field Cricket. By Dr. ERNEST CANDÈZE. Translated by N. D'ANVERS. With numerous fine Illustrations. Crown 8vo, gilt, 7s. 6d.; plain binding and edges, 5s.

*D*ANA *(R. H.) Two Years before the Mast and Twenty-Four* years After. Revised Edition, with Notes, 12mo, 6s.

Daughter (A) of Heth. By W. BLACK. Crown 8vo, 6s.

Day of My Life (A); or, Every Day Experiences at Eton. By an ETON BOY, Author of "About Some Fellows." 16mo, cloth extra, 2s. 6d. 6th Thousand.

Diane. By Mrs. MACQUOID. Crown 8vo, 6s.

Dick Cheveley: his Fortunes and Misfortunes. By W. H. G. KINGSTON. 350 pp., square 16mo, and 22 full-page Illustrations. Cloth, gilt edges, 7s. 6d.; plainer binding, plain edges, 5s.

Dick Sands, the Boy Captain. By JULES VERNE. With nearly 100 Illustrations, cloth, gilt, 10s. 6d.; plain binding and plain edges, 5s.

Dictionary (General) of Archæology and Antiquities. From the French of E. BOSC. Crown 8vo, with nearly 200 Illustrations, 10s. 6d.

Dodge (Mrs. M.) Hans Brinker; or, the Silver Skates. An entirely New Edition, with 59 Full-page and other Woodcuts. Square crown 8vo, cloth extra, 5s.; Text only, paper, 1s.

Dogs of Assize. A Legal Sketch-Book in Black and White. Containing 6 Drawings by WALTER J. ALLEN. Folio, in wrapper, 6s. 8d.

*E*IGHT *Cousins.* See ALCOTT.

Eighteenth Century Studies. Essays by F. HITCHMAN. Demy 8vo, 18s.

Elementary Education in Saxony. By J. L. BASHFORD, M.A., Trin. Coll., Camb. For Masters and Mistresses of Elementary Schools. Sewn, 1s.

Elinor Dryden. By Mrs. MACQUOID. Crown 8vo, 6s.

Embroidery (Handbook of). By L. HIGGIN. Edited by LADY MARIAN ALFORD, and published by authority of the Royal School of Art Needlework. With 16 page Illustrations, Designs for Borders, &c. Crown 8vo, 5s.

English Philosophers. Edited by IWAN MULLER, M.A., New College, Oxon. A Series of Volumes containing short biographies of the most celebrated English Philosophers, to each of whom is assigned a separate volume, giving as comprehensive and detailed a statement of his views and contributions to Philosophy as possible, explanatory rather than critical, opening with a brief biographical sketch, and concluding with a short general summary, and a bibliographical appendix. The Volumes will be issued at brief intervals, in square 16mo, 3s. 6d., containing about 200 pp. each.

The following are in the press :—

Bacon. Professor FOWLER, Professor of Logic in Oxford.

Berkeley. Professor T. H. GREEN, Professor of Moral Philosophy, Oxford.

Hamilton. Professor MONK, Professor of Moral Philosophy, Dublin. [*Ready.*

J. S. Mill. HELEN TAYLOR, Editor of "The Works of Buckle," &c.

English Philosophers (*continued*) :—

Mansel. Rev. J. H. HUCKIN, D.D., Head Master of Repton.

Adam Smith. J. A. FARRER, M.A., Author of "Primitive Manners and Customs." [*Ready*.

Hobbes. A. H. GOSSET, B.A., Fellow of New College, Oxford.

Bentham. G. E. BUCKLE, M.A., Fellow of All Souls', Oxford.

Austin. HARRY JOHNSON, B.A., late Scholar of Queen's College, Oxford.

Hartley. } E. S. BOWEN, B.A., late Scholar of New College,
James Mill. } Oxford. [*Ready*.

Shaftesbury. } Professor FOWLER.
Hutcheson. }

Arrangements are in progress for volumes on LOCKE, HUME, PALEY, REID, *&c*.

Episodes of French History. Edited, with Notes, Genealogical, Historical, and other Tables, by GUSTAVE MASSON, B.A.

    1. **Charlemagne and the Carlovingians.**

    2. **Louis XI. and the Crusades.**

    3. **Francis I. and Charles V.**

    4. **Francis I. and the Renaissance.**

The above Series is based upon M. Guizot's "History of France." Each volume is choicely Illustrated, with Maps, 2*s.* 6*d.*

Erema ; or, My Father's Sin. See BLACKMORE.

Etcher (*The*). Containing 36 Examples of the Original Etched-work of Celebrated Artists, amongst others : BIRKET FOSTER, J. E. HODGSON, R.A., COLIN HUNTER, J. P. HESELTINE, ROBERT W. MACBETH, R. S. CHATTOCK, H. R. ROBERTSON, &c., &c. Imperial 4to, cloth extra, gilt edges, 2*l.* 12*s.* 6*d.*

Eton. See "Day of my Life," "Out of School," "About Some Fellows."

Evans (*C.*) *Over the Hills and Far Away.* By C. EVANS. One Volume, crown 8vo, cloth extra, 10*s.* 6*d.*

———— *A Strange Friendship.* Crown 8vo, cloth, 5*s.*

Eve of Saint Agnes (*The*). By JOHN KEATS. Illustrated with Nineteen Etchings by CHARLES O. MURRAY. Folio, cloth extra, 21*s.* An Edition de Luxe on large paper, containing proof impressions, has been printed, and specially bound, 3*l.* 3*s.*

FARM Ballads. By WILL CARLETON. Boards, 1*s.* ; cloth, gilt edges, 1*s.* 6*d.*

Fern Paradise (*The*): *A Plea for the Culture of Ferns.* By F. G. HEATH. New Edition, entirely Rewritten, Illustrated with Eighteen full-page, numerous other Woodcuts, including 8 Plates of Ferns and Four Photographs, large post 8vo, cloth, gilt edges, 12*s.* 6*d.* Sixth Edition. In 12 Parts, sewn, 1*s.* each.

Fern World (The). By F. G. HEATH. Illustrated by Twelve Coloured Plates, giving complete Figures (Sixty-four in all) of every Species of British Fern, printed from Nature; by several full-page Engravings. Cloth, gilt, 6th Edition, 12s. 6d.

"Mr. HEATH has really given us good, well-written descriptions of our native Ferns, with indications of their habitats, the conditions under which they grow naturally, and under which they may be cultivated."—*Athenæum.*

Few (A) Hints on Proving Wills. Enlarged Edition, 1s.

First Steps in Conversational French Grammar. By F. JULIEN. Being an Introduction to "Petites Leçons de Conversation et de Grammaire," by the same Author. Fcap. 8vo, 128 pp., 1s.

Flooding of the Sahara (The). See MACKENZIE.

Food for the People; or, Lentils and other Vegetable Cookery. By E. E. ORLEBAR. Third Thousand. Small post 8vo, boards, 1s.

Fool's Errand (A). By ONE OF THE FOOLS. Author of Bricks without Straw. Crown 8vo, cloth extra, with numerous Illustrations, 8s. 6d.

Footsteps of the Master. See STOWE (Mrs. BEECHER).

Forbidden Land (A): Voyages to the Corea. By G. OPPERT. Numerous Illustrations and Maps. Demy 8vo, cloth extra, 21s.

Four Lectures on Electric Induction. Delivered at the Royal Institution, 1878-9. By J. E. H. GORDON, B.A. Cantab. With numerous Illustrations. Cloth limp, square 16mo, 3s.

Foreign Countries and the British Colonies. Edited by F. S. PULLING, M.A., Lecturer at Queen's College, Oxford, and formerly Professor at the Yorkshire College, Leeds. A Series of small Volumes descriptive of the principal Countries of the World by well-known Authors, each Country being treated of by a Writer who from Personal Knowledge is qualified to speak with authority on the Subject. The Volumes average 180 crown 8vo pages each, contain 2 Maps and Illustrations, crown 8vo, 3s. 6d.

The following is a List of the Volumes:—

Denmark and Iceland. By E. C. OTTE, Author of "Scandinavian History," &c.

Greece. By L. SERGEANT, B.A., Knight of the Hellenic Order of the Saviour, Author of "New Greece."

Switzerland. By W. A. P. COOLIDGE, M.A., Fellow of Magdalen College, Editor of *The Alpine Journal.*

Austria. By D. KAY, F.R.G.S.

Russia. By W. R. MORFILL, M.A., Oriel College, Oxford, Lecturer on the Ilchester Foundation, &c.

Persia. By Major-Gen. Sir F. J. GOLDSMID, K.C.S.I., Author of "Telegraph and Travel," &c.

Japan. By S. MOSSMAN, Author of "New Japan," &c.

Peru. By CLEMENTS H. MARKHAM, M.A., C.B.

Canada. By W. FRASER RAE, Author of "Westward by Rail," &c.

Foreign Countries (*continued*) :—

Sweden and Norway. By the Rev. F. H. WOODS, M.A., Fellow of St. John's College, Oxford.

The West Indies. By C. H. EDEN, F.R.G.S., Author of "Frozen Asia," &c.

New Zealand.

France. By Miss M. ROBERTS, Author of "The Atelier du Lys," "Mdlle. Mori," &c.

Egypt. By S. LANE POOLE, B.A., Author of "The Life of Edward Lane," &c.

Spain. By the Rev. WENTWORTH WEBSTER, M.A., Chaplain at St. Jean de Luz.

Turkey-in-Asia. By J. C. McCOAN, M.P.

Australia. By J. F. VESEY FITZGERALD, late Premier of New South Wales.

Holland. By R. L. POOLE.

Franc (*Maude Jeane*). The following form one Series, small post 8vo, in uniform cloth bindings, with gilt edges:—

———— *Emily's Choice.* 5s.

———— *Hall's Vineyard.* 4s.

———— *John's Wife : a Story of Life in South Australia.* 4s.

———— *Marian ; or, the Light of Some One's Home.* 5s.

———— *Silken Cords and Iron Fetters.* 4s.

———— *Vermont Vale.* 5s.

———— *Minnie's Mission.* 4s.

———— *Little Mercy.* 5s.

———— *Beatrice Melton's Discipline.* 4s.

Froissart (*The Boy's*). Selected from the Chronicles of England, France, Spain, &c. By SIDNEY LANIER. The Volume is fully Illustrated, and uniform with "The Boy's King Arthur." Crown 8vo, cloth, 7s. 6d.

GAMES of Patience. See CADOGAN.

Gentle Life (Queen Edition). 2 vols. in 1, small 4to, 10s. 6d.

THE GENTLE LIFE SERIES.

Price 6s. each ; or in calf extra, price 10s. 6d. ; Smaller Edition, cloth extra, 2s. 6d.

A Reprint (with the exception of "Familiar Words" and "Other People's Windows") has been issued in very neat limp cloth bindings at 2s. 6d. each.

The Gentle Life. Essays in aid of the Formation of Character of Gentlemen and Gentlewomen. 21st Edition.

"Deserves to be printed in letters of gold, and circulated in every house."— *Chambers' Journal.*

The Gentle Life Series (continued) :—

About in the World. Essays by Author of "The Gentle Life."
"It is not easy to open it at any page without finding some handy idea."—*Morning Post.*

Like unto Christ. A New Translation of Thomas à Kempis'
"De Imitatione Christi." 2nd Edition.
"Could not be presented in a more exquisite form, for a more sightly volume was never seen."—*Illustrated London News.*

Familiar Words. An Index Verborum, or Quotation Handbook. Affording an immediate Reference to Phrases and Sentences that have become embedded in the English language. 4th and enlarged Edition. 6s.
"The most extensive dictionary of quotation we have met with."—*Notes and Queries.*

Essays by Montaigne. Edited and Annotated by the Author of "The Gentle Life." With Portrait. 2nd Edition.
"We should be glad if any words of ours could help to bespeak a large circulation for this handsome attractive book."—*Illustrated Times.*

The Countess of Pembroke's Arcadia. Written by Sir PHILIP SIDNEY. Edited with Notes by Author of "The Gentle Life." 7s. 6d.
"All the best things are retained intact in Mr. Friswell's edition."—*Examiner.*

The Gentle Life. 2nd Series, 8th Edition.
"There is not a single thought in the volume that does not contribute in some measure to the formation of a true gentleman."—*Daily News.*

The Silent Hour: Essays, Original and Selected. By the Author of "The Gentle Life." 3rd Edition.
"All who possess 'The Gentle Life' should own this volume."—*Standard.*

Half-Length Portraits. Short Studies of Notable Persons. By J. HAIN FRISWELL.

Essays on English Writers, for the Self-improvement of Students in English Literature.
"To all who have neglected to read and study their native literature we would certainly suggest the volume before us as a fitting introduction."—*Examiner.*

Other People's Windows. By J. HAIN FRISWELL. 3rd Edition.
"The chapters are so lively in themselves, so mingled with shrewd views of human nature, so full of illustrative anecdotes, that the reader cannot fail to be amused."—*Morning Post.*

A Man's Thoughts. By J. HAIN FRISWELL.

German Primer. Being an Introduction to First Steps in German. By M. T. PREU. 2s. 6d.

Getting On in the World ; or, Hints on Success in Life. By W. MATHEWS, LL.D. Small post 8vo, cloth, 2s. 6d. ; gilt edges, 3s. 6d.

Gilpin's Forest Scenery. Edited by F. G. HEATH. Large post 8vo, with numerous Illustrations. Uniform with "The Fern World," 12s. 6d. In 6 monthly parts, 2s. each.

Gordon (J. E. H.). See "Four Lectures on Electric Induction," "Physical Treatise on Electricity," &c.

Gouffé. The Royal Cookery Book. By JULES GOUFFÉ; translated and adapted for English use by ALPHONSE GOUFFÉ, Head Pastrycook to her Majesty the Queen. Illustrated with large plates printed in colours. 161 Woodcuts, 8vo, cloth extra, gilt edges, 2l. 2s.

—— Domestic Edition, half-bound, 10s. 6d.

"By far the ablest and most complete work on cookery that has ever been submitted to the gastronomical world."—*Pall Mall Gazette.*

Great Artists. See "Biographies."

Great Historic Galleries of England (The). Edited by LORD RONALD GOWER, F.S.A., Trustee of the National Portrait Gallery. Illustrated by 24 large and carefully-executed *permanent* Photographs of some of the most celebrated Pictures by the Great Masters. Imperial 4to, cloth extra, gilt edges, 36s.

Great Musicians (The). A Series of Biographies of the Great Musicians. Edited by F HUEFFER.

1. **Wagner.** By the EDITOR.
2. **Weber.** By Sir JULIUS BENEDICT.
3. **Mendelssohn.** By JOSEPH BENNETT.
4. **Schubert.** By H. F. FROST.
5. **Rossini,** and the Modern Italian School. By H. SUTHERLAND EDWARDS.
6. **Marcello.** By ARRIGO BOITO.
7. **Purcell.** By H. W. CUMMINGS.

*** Dr. Hiller and other distinguished writers, both English and Foreign, have promised contributions. Each Volume is complete in itself. Small post 8vo, cloth extra, 3s.

Guizot's History of France. Translated by ROBERT BLACK. Super-royal 8vo, very numerous Full-page and other Illustrations. In 8 vols., cloth extra, gilt, each 24s.

"It supplies a want which has long been felt, and ought to be in the hands of all students of history."—*Times.*

——— ——————————— *Masson's School Edition.* The History of France from the Earliest Times to the Outbreak of the Revolution; abridged from the Translation by Robert Black, M.A., with Chronological Index, Historical and Genealogical Tables, &c. By Professor GUSTAVE MASSON, B.A., Assistant Master at Harrow School. With 24 full-page Portraits, and many other Illustrations. 1 vol., demy 8vo, 600 pp., cloth extra, 10s. 6d.

Guizot's History of England. In 3 vols. of about 500 pp. each, containing 60 to 70 Full-page and other Illustrations, cloth extra, gilt, 24s. each.

"For luxury of typography, plainness of print, and beauty of illustration, these volumes, of which but one has as yet appeared in English, will hold their own against any production of an age so luxurious as our own in everything, typography not excepted."—*Times.*

Guyon (Mde.) Life. By UPHAM. 6th Edition, crown 8vo, 6s.

HANDBOOK to the Charities of London. *See* Low's.

——— *of Embroidery ; which see.*

——— *to the Principal Schools of England.* *See* Practical.

Half-Hours of Blind Man's Holiday ; or, Summer and Winter Sketches in Black and White. By W. W. FENN, Author of "After Sundown," &c. 2 vols., cr. 8vo, 24*s.*

Hall (W. W.) How to Live Long ; or, 1408 *Health Maxims,* Physical, Mental, and Moral. By W. W. HALL, A.M., M.D. Small post 8vo, cloth, 2*s.* Second Edition.

Hans Brinker ; or, the Silver Skates. *See* DODGE.

Harper's Monthly Magazine. Published Monthly. 160 pages, fully Illustrated. 1*s.* With two Serial Novels by celebrated Authors.

"'Harper's Magazine' is so thickly sown with excellent illustrations that to count them would be a work of time ; not that it is a picture magazine, for the engravings illustrate the text after the manner seen in some of our choicest *editions de luxe.*"— *St. James's Gazette.*

"It is so pretty, so big, and so cheap. . . . An extraordinary shillingsworth— 160 large octavo pages, with over a score of articles, and more than three, times as many illustrations."—*Edinburgh Daily Review.*

"An amazing shillingsworth . . . combining choice literature of both nations."— *Nonconformist.*

Heart of Africa. Three Years' Travels and Adventures in the Unexplored Regions of Central Africa, from 1868 to 1871. By Dr. GEORG SCHWEINFURTH. Numerous Illustrations, and large Map. 2 vols., crown 8vo, cloth, 15*s.* ·

Heath (Francis George). *See* "Fern World," "Fern Paradise," "Our Woodland Trees," "Trees and Ferns," "Gilpin's Forest Scenery," "Burnham Beeches," "Sylvan Spring," &c.

Heber's (Bishop) Illustrated Edition of Hymns. With upwards of 100 beautiful Engravings. Small 4to, handsomely bound, 7*s.* 6*d.* Morocco, 18*s.* 6*d.* and 21*s.* An entirely New Edition.

Heir of Kilfinnan (The). New Story by W. H. G. KINGSTON, Author of "Snow Shoes and Canoes," &c. With Illustrations. Cloth, gilt edges, 7*s.* 6*d.* ; plainer binding, plain edges, 5*s.*

History and Handbook of Photography. Translated from the French of GASTON TISSANDIER. Edited by J. THOMSON. Imperial 16mo, over 300 pages, 70 Woodcuts, and Specimens of Prints by the best Permanent Processes. Second Edition, with an Appendix by the late Mr. HENRY FOX TALBOT. Cloth extra, 6*s.*

History of a Crime (The) ; Deposition of an Eye-witness. By VICTOR HUGO. 4 vols., crown 8vo, 42*s.* Cheap Edition, 1 vol., 6*s.*

——— *Ancient Art.* Translated from the German of JOHN WINCKELMANN, by JOHN LODGE, M.D. With very numerous Plates and Illustrations. 2 vols., 8vo, 36*s.*

——— *England.* *See* GUIZOT.

——— *France.* *See* GUIZOT.

History of Russia. See RAMBAUD.

———— *Merchant Shipping. See* LINDSAY.

———— *United States. See* BRYANT.

History and Principles of Weaving by Hand and by Power. With
  several hundred Illustrations. By ALFRED BARLOW. Royal 8vo,
  cloth extra, 1*l.* 5*s.* Second Edition.

How I Crossed Africa : from the Atlantic to the Indian Ocean,
  Through Unknown Countries ; Discovery of the Great Zambesi
  Affluents, &c.—Vol. I., The King's Rifle. Vol. II., The Coillard
  Family. By Major SERPA PINTO. With 24 full-page and 118 half-
  page and smaller Illustrations, 13 small Maps, and 1 large one.
  2 vols., demy 8vo, cloth extra, 42*s.*

How to Live Long. See HALL.

How to get Strong and how to Stay so. By WILLIAM BLAIKIE.
  A Manual of Rational, Physical, Gymnastic, and other Exercises.
  With Illustrations, small post 8vo, 5*s.*

Hugo (Victor) "Ninety-Three." Illustrated. Crown 8vo, 6*s.*

———— *Toilers of the Sea.* Crown 8vo. Illustrated, 6*s.*; fancy
  boards, 2*s.*; cloth, 2*s.* 6*d.*; On large paper with all the original
  Illustrations, 10*s.* 6*d.*

————. *See* "History of a Crime."

Hundred Greatest Men (The). 8 portfolios, 21*s.* each, or 4
  vols., half morocco, gilt edges, 12 guineas, containing 15 to 20
  Portraits each. See below.

  "Messrs. SAMPSON LOW & Co. are about to issue an important 'International'
  work, entitled, 'THE HUNDRED GREATEST MEN;' being the Lives and
  Portraits of the 100 Greatest Men of History, divided into Eight Classes, each Class
  to form a Monthly Quarto Volume. The Introductions to the volumes are to be
  written by recognized authorities on the different subjects, the English contributors
  being DEAN STANLEY, Mr. MATTHEW ARNOLD, Mr. FROUDE, and Professor MAX
  MÜLLER : in Germany, Professor HELMHOLTZ ; in France, MM. TAINE and
  RENAN ; and in America, Mr. EMERSON. The Portraits are to be Reproductions
  from fine and rare Steel Engravings."—*Academy.*

Hygiene and Public Health (A Treatise on). Edited by A. H.
  BUCK, M.D. Illustrated by numerous Wood Engravings. In 2
  royal 8vo vols., cloth, one guinea each.

Hymnal Companion to Book of Common Prayer. See
  BICKERSTETH.

ILLUSTRATED Text-Books of Art-Education. Edited by
  EDWARD J. POYNTER, R.A. Each Volume contains numerous Illus-
  trations, and is strongly bound for the use of Students, price 5*s.* The
  Volumes now ready are :—

PAINTING.

Classic and Italian. By PERCY | German, Flemish, and Dutch.
  R. HEAD. With 50 Illustrations, | French and Spanish.
  5*s.* | English and American.

Illustrated Text-Books (continued) :—

ARCHITECTURE.

Classic and Early Christian.
Gothic and Renaissance. By T. ROGER SMITH. With 50 Illustrations, 5*s.*

SCULPTURE.

Antique: Egyptian and Greek. | **Renaissance and Modern.**

ORNAMENT.

Decoration in Colour. | **Architectural Ornament.**

Illustrations of China and its People. By J. THOMPSON, F.R.G.S. Four Volumes, imperial 4to, each 3*l.* 3*s.*

In my Indian Garden. By PHIL ROBINSON, Author of " Under the Punkah." With a Preface by EDWIN ARNOLD, M.A., C.S.I., &c. Crown 8vo, limp cloth, 3*s.* 6*d.*

Involuntary Voyage (An). Showing how a Frenchman who abhorred the Sea was most unwillingly and by a series of accidents driven round the World. Numerous Illustrations. Square crown 8vo, cloth extra, 7*s.* 6*d.*; plainer binding, plain edges, 5*s.*

Irish Bar. Comprising Anecdotes, Bon-Mots, and Biographical Sketches of the Bench and Bar of Ireland. By J. RODERICK O'FLANAGAN, Barrister-at-Law. Crown 8vo, 12*s.* Second Edition.

Irish Land Question, and English Public Opinion (The). With a Supplement on Griffith's Valuation. By R. BARRY O'BRIEN, Author of " The Parliamentary History of the Irish Land Question." Fcap. 8vo, cloth, 2*s.*

Irving (Washington). Complete Library Edition of his Works in 27 Vols., Copyright, Unabridged, and with the Author's Latest Revisions, called the " Geoffrey Crayon " Edition, handsomely printed in large square 8vo, on superfine laid paper, and each volume, of about 500 pages, will be fully Illustrated. 12*s.* 6*d.* per vol. *See also* " Little Britain."

JACK and Jill. By Miss ALCOTT. Small post 8vo, cloth, gilt edges, 5*s.* With numerous Illustrations.

John Holdsworth, Chief Mate. By W. CLARKE RUSSELL, Author of " Wreck of the Grosvenor." Crown 8vo, 6*s.*

KINGSTON (W. H. G.). *See* " Snow-Shoes," " Child of the Cavern," " Two Supercargoes," " With Axe and Rifle," " Begum's Fortune," " Heir of Kilfinnan," " Dick Cheveley." Each vol., with very numerous Illustrations, square crown 16mo, gilt edges, 7*s.* 6*d.*; plainer binding, plain edges, 5*s.*

LADY Silverdale's Sweetheart. 6s. *See* BLACK.

Lenten Meditations. In Two Series, each complete in itself.
By the Rev. CLAUDE BOSANQUET, Author of "Blossoms from the
King's Garden." 16mo, cloth, First Series, 1s. 6d. ; Second Series, 2s.

Library of Religious Poetry. A Collection of the Best Poems
of all Ages and Tongues. With Biographical and Literary Notes.
Edited by PHILIP SCHAFF, D.D., LL.D., and ARTHUR GILMAN,
M.A. Royal 8vo, pp. 1036, cloth extra, gilt edges, 21s.

Life and Letters of the Honourable Charles Sumner (The).
2 vols., royal 8vo, cloth. Second Edition, 36s.

Lindsay (W. S.) History of Merchant Shipping and Ancient
Commerce. Over 150 Illustrations, Maps, and Charts. In 4 vols.,
demy 8vo, cloth extra. Vols. 1 and 2, 21s. ; vols. 3 and 4, 24s. each.

Little Britain ; together with *The Spectre Bridegroom,* and *A*
Legend of Sleepy Hollow. By WASHINGTON IRVING. An entirely
New *Edition de luxe,* specially suitable for Presentation. Illustrated
by 120 very fine Engravings on Wood, by Mr. J. D. COOPER.
Designed by Mr. CHARLES O. MURRAY. Square crown 8vo, cloth
extra, gilt edges, 10s. 6d.

Little King ; or, the Taming of a Young Russian Count. By
S. BLANDY. 64 Illustrations. Crown 8vo, gilt edges, 7s. 6d. ; plainer
binding, 5s.

Little Mercy ; or, For Better for Worse. By MAUDE JEANNE
FRANC, Author of "Marian," "Vermont Vale," &c., &c. Small
post 8vo, cloth extra, 4s. Second Edition.

Lost Sir Massingberd. New Edition, crown 8vo, boards, coloured
wrapper, 2s.

Low's German Series—

1. **The Illustrated German Primer.** Being the easiest introduction
   to the study of German for all beginners. 1s.
2. **The Children's own German Book.** A Selection of Amusing
   and Instructive Stories in Prose. Edited by Dr. A. L. MEISSNER.
   Small post 8vo, cloth, 1s. 6d.
3. **The First German Reader, for Children from Ten to**
   Fourteen. Edited by Dr. A. L. MEISSNER. Small post 8vo,
   cloth, 1s. 6d.
4. **The Second German Reader.** Edited by Dr. A. L. MEISSNER.
   Small post 8vo, cloth, 1s. 6d.

   Buchheim's Deutsche Prosa. Two Volumes, sold separately :—

5. **Schiller's Prosa.** Containing Selections from the Prose Works
   of Schiller, with Notes for English Students. By Dr. BUCHHEIM.
   Small post 8vo, 2s. 6d.
6. **Goethe's Prosa.** Selections from the Prose Works of Goethe,
   with Notes for English Students. By Dr. BUCHHEIM. Small
   post 8vo, 3s. 6d.

Low's International Series of Toy Books. 6*d.* each ; or
Mounted on Linen, 1*s.*

  1. **Little Fred and his Fiddle,** from Asbjörnsen's "Norwegian
     Fairy Tales."

  2. **The Lad and the North Wind,**   ditto.

  3. **The Pancake,**   ditto.

  4. **The Little Match Girl,** from H. C. Andersen's "Danish
     Fairy Tales."

  5. **The Emperor's New Clothes,**   ditto.

  6. **The Gallant Tin Soldier,**   ditto.

    The above in 1 vol., cloth extra, gilt edges, with the whole 36
Coloured Illustrations, 5*s.*

Low's Standard Library of Travel and Adventure. Crown 8vo,
bound uniformly in cloth extra, price 7*s.* 6*d.*

  1. **The Great Lone Land.** By Major W. F. BUTLER, C.B.

  2. **The Wild North Land.** By Major W. F. BUTLER, C.B.

  3. **How I found Livingstone.** By H. M. STANLEY.

  4. **The Threshold of the Unknown Region.** By C. R. MARK-
     HAM. (4th Edition, with Additional Chapters, 10*s.* 6*d.*)

  5. **A Whaling Cruise to Baffin's Bay and the Gulf of Boothia.**
     By A. H. MARKHAM.

  6. **Campaigning on the Oxus.** By J. A. MacGAHAN.

  7. **Akim-foo: the History of a Failure.** By MAJOR W. F.
     BUTLER, C.B.

  8. **Ocean to Ocean.** By the Rev. GEORGE M. GRANT. With
     Illustrations.

  9. **Cruise of the Challenger.** By W. J. J. SPRY, R.N.

 10. **Schweinfurth's Heart of Africa.** 2 vols., 15*s.*

 11. **Through the Dark Continent.** By H. M. STANLEY. 1 vol.,
     12*s.* 6*d.*

Low's Standard Novels. Crown 8vo, 6*s.* each, cloth extra.

  My Lady Greensleeves. By HELEN MATHERS, Authoress of
    "Comin' through the Rye," "Cherry Ripe," &c.

  Three Feathers. By WILLIAM BLACK.

  A Daughter of Heth. 13th Edition. By W. BLACK. With
    Frontispiece by F. WALKER, A.R.A.

  Kilmeny. A Novel. By W. BLACK.

  In Silk Attire. By W. BLACK.

  Lady Silverdale's Sweetheart. By W. BLACK.

  History of a Crime: The Story of the Coup d'Etat. By VICTOR
    HUGO.

Low's Standard Novels (*continued*) :—

Alice Lorraine. By R. D. BLACKMORE.

Lorna Doone. By R. D. BLACKMORE. 8th Edition.

Cradock Nowell. By R. D. BLACKMORE.

Clara Vaughan. By R. D. BLACKMORE.

Cripps the Carrier. By R. D. BLACKMORE.

Erema; or, My Father's Sin. By R. D. BLACKMORE.

Mary Anerley. By R. D. BLACKMORE.

Innocent. By Mrs. OLIPHANT. Eight Illustrations.

Work. A Story of Experience. By LOUISA M. ALCOTT. Illustrations. *See also* Rose Library.

The Afghan Knife. By R. A. STERNDALE, Author of "Seonee."

A French Heiress in her own Chateau. By the Author of "One Only," "Constantia," &c. Six Illustrations.

Ninety-Three. By VICTOR HUGO. Numerous Illustrations.

My Wife and I. By Mrs. BEECHER STOWE.

Wreck of the Grosvenor. By W. CLARK RUSSELL.

John Holdsworth (Chief Mate). By W. CLARK RUSSELL.

Elinor Dryden. By Mrs. MACQUOID.

Diane. By Mrs. MACQUOID.

Poganuc People, Their Loves and Lives. By Mrs. BEECHER STOWE.

A Golden Sorrow. By Mrs. CASHEL HOEY.

A Story of the Dragonnades; or, Asylum Christi. By the Rev. E. GILLIAT, M.A.

Low's Handbook to the Charities of London. Edited and revised to date by C. MACKESON, F.S.S., Editor of "A Guide to the Churches of London and its Suburbs," &c. Paper, 1*s.* ; cloth, 1*s.* 6*d.*

MACGAHAN (*J. A.*) *Campaigning on the Oxus, and the Fall of Khiva.* With Map and numerous Illustrations, 4th Edition, small post 8vo, cloth extra, 7*s.* 6*d.*

Macgregor (*John*) *"Rob Roy" on the Baltic.* 3rd Edition, small post 8vo, 2*s.* 6*d.* ; cloth, gilt edges, 3*s.* 6*d.*

——— *A Thousand Miles in the "Rob Roy" Canoe.* 11th Edition, small post 8vo, 2*s.* 6*d.* ; cloth, gilt edges, 3*s.* 6*d.*

——— *Description of the "Rob Roy" Canoe,* with Plans, &c., 1*s.*

——— *The Voyage Alone in the Yawl "Rob Roy."* New Edition, thoroughly revised, with additions, small post 8vo, 5*s.* ; boards, 2*s.* 6*d.*

Mackenzie (D.) *The Flooding of the Sahara.* By DONALD MACKENZIE. 8vo, cloth extra, with Illustrations, 10s. 6d.

Macquoid (Mrs.) Elinor Dryden. Crown 8vo, cloth, 6s.

———— *Diane.* Crown 8vo, 6s.

Magazine. See HARPER.

Markham (C. R.) The Threshold of the Unknown Region. Crown 8vo, with Four Maps, 4th Edition. Cloth extra, 10s. 6d.

Maury (Commander) Physical Geography of the Sea, and its Meteorology. Being a Reconstruction and Enlargement of his former Work, with Charts and Diagrams. New Edition, crown 8vo, 6s.

Memoirs of Count Miot de Melito. 2 vols., demy 8vo, 36s.

Memoirs of Madame de Rémusat, 1802—1808. By her Grandson, M. PAUL DE RÉMUSAT; Senator. Translated by Mrs. CASHEL HOEY and Mr. JOHN LILLIE. 4th Edition, cloth extra. This work was written by Madame de Rémusat during the time she was living on the most intimate terms with the Empress Josephine, and is full of revelations respecting the private life of Bonaparte, and of men and politics of the first years of the century. Revelations which have already created a great sensation in Paris. 8vo, 2 vols., 32s.

Menus (366, one for each day of the year). Translated from the French of COUNT BRISSE, by Mrs. MATTHEW CLARKE. Crown 8vo, 10s. 6d.

Men of Mark : a Gallery of Contemporary Portraits of the most Eminent Men of the Day taken from Life, especially for this publication, price 1s. 6d. monthly. Vols. I., II., III., IV., and V., handsomely bound, cloth, gilt edges, 25s. each.

Mendelssohn Family (The). Translated from the German of E. BOCK. Demy 8vo, 16s.

Michael Strogoff. 10s. 6d. and 5s. *See* VERNE.

Mitford (Miss). See "Our Village."

Military Maxims. By CAPTAIN B. TERLING. Medium 16mo, in roan case, with pencil for the pocket, 10s. 6d.

Mountain and Prairie : a Journey from Victoria to Winnipeg, viâ Peace River Pass. By the Rev. DANIEL M. GORDON, B.D., Ottawa. Small post 8vo, with Maps and Illustrations, cloth extra, 8s. 6d.

Music. See "Great Musicians."

My Lady Greensleeves. By HELEN MATHERS, Authoress of "Comin' through the Rye," "Cherry Ripe," &c. 1 vol. edition, crown 8vo, cloth, 6s.

Mysterious Island. By JULES VERNE. 3 vols., imperial 16mo. 150 Illustrations, cloth gilt, 3s. 6d. each; elaborately bound, gilt edges, 7s. 6d. each. Cheap Edition, with some of the Illustrations, cloth, gilt, 2s.; paper, 1s. each.

NATIONAL Music of the World. By the late HENRY F. CHORLEY. Edited by H. G. HEWLETT. Crown 8vo, cloth, 8s. 6d.

Naval Brigade in South Africa (The). By HENRY F. NORBURY, C.B., R.N. Crown 8vo, cloth extra, 10s. 6d.

New Child's Play (A). Sixteen Drawings by E. V. B. Beautifully printed in colours, 4to, cloth extra, 12s. 6d.

New Guinea (A Few Months in). By OCTAVIUS C. STONE, F.R.G.S. With numerous Illustrations from the Author's own Drawings. Crown 8vo, cloth, 12s.

———— *What I did and what I saw.* By L. M. D'ALBERTIS, Officer of the Order of the Crown of Italy, Honorary Member and Gold Medallist of the I.R.G.S., C.M.Z.S., &c., &c. In 2 vols., demy 8vo, cloth extra, with Maps, Coloured Plates, and numerous very fine Woodcut Illustrations, 42s.

New Ireland. By A. M. SULLIVAN, M.P. for Louth. 2 vols., demy 8vo, 30s. Cheaper Edition, 1 vol., crown 8vo, 8s. 6d.

New Novels. Crown 8vo, cloth, 10s. 6d. per vol. :—

Mary Marston. By GEORGE MACDONALD. 3 vols. Third Edition.
Sarah de Beranger. By JEAN INGELOW. 3 vols.
Don John. By JEAN INGELOW. 3 vols.
Sunrise: A Story of these Times. By WILLIAM BLACK. 3 vols.
A Sailor's Sweetheart. By W. CLARK RUSSELL, Author of "The Wreck of the Grosvenor," "John Holdsworth," &c. 3 vols.
Lisa Lena. By EDWARD JENKINS, Author of "Ginx's Baby." 2 vols.
A Plot of the Present Day. By KATE HOPE. 3 vols.
Black Abbey. By M. CROMMELIN, Author of "Queenie," &c. 3 vols.
Flower o' the Broom. By the Author of "Rare Pale Margaret," 3 vols.
The Grandidiers: A Tale of Berlin. Translated from the German by Captain WM. SAVILE. 3 vols.
Errant: A Life Story of Latter-Day Chivalry. By PERCY GREG, Author of "Across the Zodiac," &c. 3 vols.
Fancy Free. By C. GIBBON. 3 vols.
The Stillwater Tragedy. By J. B. ALDRICH.
Prince Fortune and Prince Fatal. By Mrs. CARRINGTON, Author of "My Cousin Maurice," &c. 3 vols.

New Novels (*continued*) :—

 An English Squire. By C. B. COLERIDGE, Author of "Lady Betty," "Hanbury Wills," &c. 3 vols.

 Christowell. By R. D. BLACKMORE. 3 vols.

 Mr. Caroll. By Miss SEGUIN. 3 vols.

 David Broome, Artist. By Miss O'REILLY. 3 vols.

 Braes of Yarrow. By CHAS. GIBBON. 3 vols.

Nice and Her Neighbours. By the Rev. CANON HOLE, Author of "A Book about Roses," "A Little Tour in Ireland," &c. Small 4to, with numerous choice Illustrations, 12s. 6d.

Noble Words and Noble Deeds. From the French of E. MULLER. Containing many Full-page Illustrations by PHILIPPOTEAUX. Square imperial 16mo, cloth extra, 7s. 6d. ; plainer binding, plain edges, 5s.

North American Review (*The*). Monthly, price 2s. 6d.

Nothing to Wear ; and Two Millions. By W. A. BUTLER. New Edition. Small post 8vo, in stiff coloured wrapper, 1s.

Nursery Playmates (*Prince of*). 217 Coloured pictures for Children by eminent Artists. Folio, in coloured boards, 6s.

OBERAMMERGAU Passion Play. See "Art in the Mountains."

O'Brien. See "Parliamentary History" and "Irish Land Question."

Old-Fashioned Girl. See ALCOTT.

On Horseback through Asia Minor. By Capt. FRED BURNABY, Royal Horse Guards, Author of "A Ride to Khiva." 2 vols., 8vo, with three Maps and Portrait of Author, 6th Edition, 38s. ; Cheaper Edition, crown 8vo, 10s. 6d.

Our Little Ones in Heaven. Edited by the Rev. H. ROBBINS. With Frontispiece after Sir JOSHUA REYNOLDS. Fcap., cloth extra, New Edition—the 3rd, with Illustrations, 5s.

Our Village. By MARY RUSSELL MITFORD. Illustrated with Frontispiece Steel Engraving, and 12 full-page and 157 smaller Cuts of Figure Subjects and Scenes. Crown 4to, cloth, gilt edges, 21s.

Our Woodland Trees. By F. G. HEATH. Large post 8vo, cloth, gilt edges, uniform with "Fern World" and "Fern Paradise," by the same Author. 8 Coloured Plates (showing leaves of every British Tree) and 20 Woodcuts, cloth, gilt edges, 12s. 6d. Third Edition.

PAINTERS of All Schools. By LOUIS VIARDOT, and other
Writers. 500 pp., super-royal 8vo, 20 Full-page and 70 smaller
Engravings, cloth extra, 25*s.* A New Edition is issued in Half-
crown parts, with fifty additional portraits, cloth, gilt edges, 31*s.* 6*d.*

Painting (A Short History of the British School of). By
GEO. H. SHEPHERD. Post 8vo, cloth, 3*s.* 6*d.*

Palliser (Mrs.) A History of Lace, from the Earliest Period.
A New and Revised Edition, with additional cuts and text, upwards
of 100 Illustrations and coloured Designs. 1 vol., 8vo, 1*l.* 1*s.*

—————— *Historic Devices, Badges, and War Cries.* 8vo, 1*l.* 1*s.*

—————— *The China Collector's Pocket Companion.* With upwards of 1000 Illustrations of Marks and Monograms. 2nd Edition,
with Additions. Small post 8vo, limp cloth, 5*s.*

Parliamentary History of the Irish Land Question (The). From
1829 to 1869, and the Origin and Results of the Ulster Custom. By
R. BARRY O'BRIEN, Barrister-at-Law, Author of "The Irish Land
Question and English Public Opinion." 3rd Edition, corrected and
revised, with additional matter. Post 8vo, cloth extra, 6*s.*
   The Right Hon. W. E. GLADSTONE, M.P., in a Letter to the Author, says:—
"I thank you for kindly sending me your work, and I hope that the sad and dis-
creditable story which you have told so well in your narrative of the Irish Land
Question may be useful at a period when we have more than ever of reason to desire
that it should be thoroughly understood."

Pathways of Palestine : a Descriptive Tour through the Holy
Land. By the Rev. CANON TRISTRAM. Illustrated with 44 per-
manent Photographs. (The Photographs are large, and most perfect
Specimens of the Art.) Published in 22 Monthly Parts, 4to, in
Wrapper, 2*s.* 6*d.* each.
   ". . . The Photographs which illustrate these pages may justly claim, as works
of art, to be the most admirably executed views which have been produced. . . .
   "As the writer is on the point of making a fourth visit of exploration to the
country, any new discoveries which come under observation will be at once incor-
porated in this work."

Peasant Life in the West of England. By FRANCIS GEORGE
HEATH, Author of "Sylvan Spring," "The Fern World." Crown
8vo, about 350 pp., 10*s.* 6*d.*

Petites Leçons de Conversation et de Grammaire: Oral and
Conversational Method ; being Lessons introducing the most Useful
Topics of Conversation, upon an entirely new principle, &c. By
F. JULIEN, French Master at King Edward the Sixth's School,
Birmingham. Author of "The Student's French Examiner," "First
Steps in Conversational French Grammar," which see.

Phillips (L.) Dictionary of Biographical Reference. 8vo,
1*l.* 11*s.* 6*d.*

Photography (History and Handbook of). See TISSANDIER.

Physical Treatise on Electricity and Magnetism. By J. E. H. GORDON, B.A. With about 200 coloured, full-page, and other Illustrations. Among the newer portions of the work may be enumerated : All the more recent investigations on Striæ by Spottiswoode, De la Rue, Moulton, &c., an account of Mr. Crooke's recent researches ; full descriptions and pictures of all the modern Magnetic Survey Instruments now used at Kew Observatory ; full accounts of all the modern work on Specific Inductive Capacity, and of the more recent determination of the ratio of Electric units (v). In respect to the number and beauty of the Illustrations, the work is quite unique. 2 vols., 8vo, 36s.

Pinto (Major Serpa). *See* " How I Crossed Africa."

Plutarch's Lives. An Entirely New and Library Edition. Edited by A. H. CLOUGH, Esq. 5 vols., 8vo, 2l. 10s.; half-morocco, gilt top, 3l. Also in 1 vol., royal 8vo, 800 pp., cloth extra, 18s.; half-bound, 21s.

Poems of the Inner Life. A New Edition, Revised, with many additional Poems. Small post 8vo, cloth, 5s.

Poganuc People: their Loves and Lives. By Mrs. BEECHER STOWE. Crown 8vo, cloth, 6s.

Polar Expeditions. *See* KOLDEWEY, MARKHAM, MACGAHAN, and NARES.

Poynter (Edward J., R.A.). *See* " Illustrated Text-books."

Practical (A) Handbook to the Principal Schools of England. By C. E. PASCOE. New Edition, crown 8vo, cloth extra, 3s. 6d.

Prejevalsky (N. M.) From Kulja, across the Tian Shan to Lobnor. Translated by E. DELMAR MORGAN, F.R.G.S. Demy 8vo, with a Map. 16s.

Primitive Folk Moots ; or, Open-Air Assemblies in Britain. By GEORGE LAURENCE GOMME, F.S.A., Honorary Secretary to the Folk-Lore Society, Author of " Index of Municipal Offices." 1 vol., crown 8vo, cloth, 12s.
   This work deals with an earlier phase of the history of English Institutions than has yet been attempted.

Publishers' Circular (The), and General Record of British and Foreign Literature. Published on the 1st and 15th of every Month, 3d.

Pyrenees (The). By HENRY BLACKBURN. With 100 Illustrations by GUSTAVE DORE, a New Map of Routes, and Information for Travellers, corrected to 1881. With a description of Lourdes in 1880. Crown 8vo, cloth extra, 7s. 6d.

RAMBAUD (Alfred). History of Russia, from its Origin to the Year 1877. With Six Maps. Translated by Mrs. L. B. 1/1.2 vols., demy 8vo, cloth extra, 38*s.*

Recollections of Writers. By CHARLES and MARY COWDEN CLARKE. Authors of "The Concordance to Shakespeare," &c. ; with Letters of CHARLES LAMB, LEIGH HUNT, DOUGLAS JERROLD, and CHARLES DICKENS ; and a Preface by MARY COWDEN CLARKE. Crown 8vo, cloth, 10*s.* 6*d.* .

Rémusat (Madame de). *See* "Memoirs of."

Robinson (Phil). *See* "In my Indian Garden," "Under the Punkah."

Rochefoucauld's Reflections. Bayard Series, 2*s.* 6*d.*

Rogers (S.) Pleasures of Memory. See "Choice Editions of Choice Books." 2*s.* 6*d.*

Rose in Bloom. See ALCOTT.

The Rose Library. Popular Literature of all countries. Each volume, 1*s.* ; cloth, 2*s.* 6*d.* Many of the Volumes are Illustrated—

1. **Sea-Gull Rock.** By JULES SANDEAU. Illustrated.
2. **Little Women.** By LOUISA M. ALCOTT.
3. **Little Women Wedded.** Forming a Sequel to "Little Women."
4. **The House on Wheels.** By MADAME DE STOLZ. Illustrated.
5. **Little Men.** By LOUISA M. ALCOTT. Dble. vol., 2*s.* ; cloth, 3*s.* 6*d.*
6. **The Old-Fashioned Girl.** By LOUISA M. ALCOTT. Double vol., 2*s.* ; cloth, 3*s.* 6*d.*
7. **The Mistress of the Manse.** By J. G. HOLLAND.
8. **Timothy Titcomb's Letters to Young People, Single and Married.**
9. **Undine, and the Two Captains.** By Baron DE LA MOTTE FOUQUÉ. A New Translation by F. E. BUNNETT. Illustrated.
10. **Draxy Miller's Dowry, and the Elder's Wife.** By SAXE HOLM.
11. **The Four Gold Pieces.** By Madame GOURAUD. Numerous Illustrations.
12. **Work.** A Story of Experience. First Portion. By LOUISA M. ALCOTT.
13. **Beginning Again.** Being a Continuation of "Work." By LOUISA M. ALCOTT.
14. **Picciola; or, the Prison Flower.** By X. B. SAINTINE. Numerous Graphic Illustrations.

The Rose Library (*continued*) :—

15. **Robert's Holidays.** Illustrated.
16. **The Two Children of St. Domingo.** Numerous Illustrations.
17. **Aunt Jo's Scrap Bag.**
18. **Stowe (Mrs. H. B.) The Pearl of Orr's Island.**
19. —— **The Minister's Wooing.**
20. —— **Betty's Bright Idea.**
21. —— **The Ghost in the Mill.**
22. —— **Captain Kidd's Money.**
23. —— **We and our Neighbours.** Double vol., *2s.*
24. —— **My Wife and I.** Double vol., *2s.* ; cloth, gilt, *3s. 6d.*
25. **Hans Brinker**; or, the **Silver Skates.**
26. **Lowell's My Study Window.**
27. **Holmes (O. W.) The Guardian Angel.**
28. **Warner (C. D.) My Summer in a Garden.**
29. **Hitherto.** By the Author of "The Gayworthys." 2 vols., *1s.* each.
30. **Helen's Babies.** By their Latest Victim.
31. **The Barton Experiment.** By the Author of "Helen's Babies."
32. **Dred.** By Mrs. BEECHER STOWE. Double vol., *2s.* ; cloth, gilt, *3s. 6d.*
33. **Warner (C. D.) In the Wilderness.**
34. **Six to One.** A Seaside Story.
35. **Nothing to Wear, and Two Millions.**
36. **Farm Ballads.** By WILL CARLETON.

Russell (*W. Clarke*). *See* "A Sailor's Sweetheart," 3 vols., 31*s. 6d.* ; "Wreck of the Grosvenor," 6*s.* ; "John Holdsworth (Chief Mate)," 6*s.*

Russell (*W. H., LL.D.*) *The Tour of the Prince of Wales in India.* By W. H. RUSSELL, LL.D. Fully Illustrated by SYDNEY P. HALL, M.A. Super-royal 8vo, cloth extra, gilt edges, 52*s. 6d.*; Large Paper Edition, 84*s.*

*S*ANCTA *Christina : a Story of the First Century.* By ELEANOR E. ORLEBAR. With a Preface by the Bishop of Winchester. Small post 8vo, cloth extra, 5*s.*

Seonee : Sporting in the Satpura Range of Central India, and in the Valley of the Nerbudda. By R. A. STERNDALE, F.R.G.S. 8vo, with numerous Illustrations, 21*s.*

Seven Years in South Africa : Travels, Researches, and Hunting Adventures between the Diamond-Fields and the Zambesi (1872—1879). By Dr. EMIL HOLUB. With over 100 Original Illustrations and 4 Maps. In 2 vols., demy 8vo, cloth extra, 42*s.*

Serpent Charmer (The): a Tale of the Indian Mutiny. By
LOUIS ROUSSELET, Author of "India and its Native Princes."
Numerous Illustrations. Crown 8vo, cloth extra, gilt edges, 7*s.* 6*d.* ;
plainer binding, 5*s.*

Shakespeare (The Boudoir). Edited by HENRY CUNDELL.
Carefully bracketted for reading aloud ; freed from all objectionable
matter, and altogether free from notes. Price 2*s.* 6*d.* each volume,
cloth extra, gilt edges. Contents :—Vol I., Cymbeline—Merchant of
Venice. Each play separately, paper cover, 1*s.* Vol. II., As You
Like It—King Lear—Much Ado about Nothing. Vol. III., Romeo
and Juliet—Twelfth Night—King John. The latter six plays separately, paper cover, 9*d.*

Shakespeare Key (The). Forming a Companion to "The
Complete Concordance to Shakespeare." By CHARLES and MARY
COWDEN CLARKE. Demy 8vo, 800 pp., 21*s.*

Shooting: its Appliances, Practice, and Purpose. By JAMES
DALZIEL DOUGALL, F.S.A., F.Z.A., Author of "Scottish Field
Sports," &c. Crown 8vo, cloth extra, 10*s.* 6*d.*

"The book is admirable in every way. . . . . We wish it every success."—*Globe.*
"A very complete treatise. . . . . Likely to take high rank as an authority on
shooting."—*Daily News.*

Silent Hour (The). *See* "Gentle Life Series."

Silver Pitchers. *See* ALCOTT.

Simon (Jules). *See* "Government of M. Thiers."

Six to One. A Seaside Story. 16mo, boards, 1*s.*

Smith (G.) Assyrian Explorations and Discoveries. By the late
GEORGE SMITH. Illustrated by Photographs and Woodcuts. Demy
8vo, 6th Edition, 18*s.*

——— *The Chaldean Account of Genesis.* By the late
G. SMITH, of the Department of Oriental Antiquities, British Museum.
With many Illustrations. Demy 8vo, cloth extra, 6th Edition, 16*s.*

——— An entirely New Edition, completely revised and rewritten by the Rev. PROFESSOR SAYCE, Queen's College, Oxford.
Demy 8vo, 18*s.*

Snow-Shoes and Canoes ; or, the Adventures of a Fur-Hunter
in the Hudson's Bay Territory. By W. H. G. KINGSTON. 2nd
Edition. With numerous Illustrations. Square crown 8vo, cloth
extra, gilt edges, 7*s.* 6*d.* ; plainer binding, 5*s.*

Songs and Etchings in Shade and Sunshine. By J. E. G. Illustrated with 44 Etchings. Small 4to, cloth, gilt tops, 25*s.*

South African Campaign, 1879 (*The*). Compiled by J. P. MACKINNON (formerly 72nd Highlanders), and S. H. SHADBOLT; and dedicated, by permission, to Field-Marshal H.R.H. The Duke of Cambridge. 4to, handsomely bound in cloth extra, 2*l.* 10*s.*

South Kensington Museum. Published, with the sanction of the Science and Art Department, in Monthly Parts, each containing 8 Plates, price 1*s.* Volume I., containing 12 numbers, handsomely bound, 16*s.*

Stanley (H. M.) How I Found Livingstone. Crown 8vo, cloth extra, 7*s.* 6*d.*; large Paper Edition, 10*s.* 6*d.*

———— *"My Kalulu," Prince, King, and Slave.* A Story from Central Africa. Crown 8vo, about 430 pp., with numerous graphic Illustrations, after Original Designs by the Author. Cloth, 7*s.* 6*d.*

———— *Coomassie and Magdala.* A Story of Two British Campaigns in Africa. Demy 8vo, with Maps and Illustrations, 16*s.*

———— *Through the Dark Continent,* which see.

Story of a Mountain (The). By E. RECLUS. Translated by BERTHA NESS. 8vo, with Illustrations, cloth extra, gilt edges, 7*s.* 6*d.*

Story of a Soldier's Life (The); or, Peace, War, and Mutiny. By Lieut.-General JOHN ALEXANDER EWART, C.B., Aide-de-Camp to the Queen from 1859 to 1872. 2 vols., demy 8vo, with Illustrations.

Story of the Zulu Campaign (The). By Major ASHE (late King's Dragoon Guards), and Captain the Hon. E. V. WYATT-EDGELL (late 17th Lancers, killed at Ulundi). Dedicated by special permission to Her Imperial Highness the Empress Eugénie. 8vo, 16*s.*

Story without an End. From the German of Carové, by the late Mrs. SARAH T. AUSTIN. Crown 4to, with 15 Exquisite Drawings by E. V. B., printed in Colours in Fac-simile of the original Water Colours; and numerous other Illustrations. New Edition, 7*s.* 6*d.*

———— square 4to, with Illustrations by HARVEY. 2*s.* 6*d.*

Stowe (Mrs. Beecher) Dred. Cheap Edition, boards, 2*s.* Cloth, gilt edges, 3*s.* 6*d.*

Stowe (*Mrs. Beecher*) *Footsteps of the Master.* With Illustrations and red borders. Small post 8vo, cloth extra, 6s.

—————— *Geography,* with 60 Illustrations. Square cloth, 4s. 6d.

—————— *Little Foxes.* Cheap Edition, 1s.; Library Edition, 4s. 6d.

—————— *Betty's Bright Idea.* 1s.

—————— *My Wife and I; or, Harry Henderson's History.* Small post 8vo, cloth extra, 6s.*

—————— *Minister's Wooing.* 5s.; Copyright Series, 1s. 6d.; cl., 2s.*

—————— *Old Town Folk.* 6s.; Cheap Edition, 2s. 6d.

—————— *Old Town Fireside Stories.* Cloth extra, 3s. 6d.

—————— *Our Folks at Poganuc.* 10s. 6d.

—————— *We and our Neighbours.* 1 vol., small post 8vo, 6s. Sequel to "My Wife and I."*

—————— *Pink and White Tyranny.* Small post 8vo, 3s. 6d. Cheap Edition, 1s. 6d. and 2s.

—————— *Queer Little People.* 1s.; cloth, 2s.

—————— *Chimney Corner.* 1s.; cloth, 1s. 6d.

—————— *The Pearl of Orr's Island.* Crown 8vo, 5s.*

—————— *Little Pussey Willow.* Fcap., 2s.

—————— *Woman in Sacred History.* Illustrated with 15 Chromo-lithographs and about 200 pages of Letterpress. Dem 4to, cloth extra, gilt edges, 25s.

Student's French Examiner. By F. Julien, Author of " Petites Leçons de Conversation et de Grammaire." Square crown 8vo, cloth, 2s

Studies in German Literature. By Bayard Taylor. Edited by Marie Taylor. With an Introduction by the Hon. George H. Boker. 8vo, cloth extra, 10s. 6d.

* *See also* Rose Library.

Studies in the Theory of Descent. By Dr. AUG. WEISMANN, Professor in the University of Freiburg. Translated and edited by RAPHAEL MELDOLA, F.C.S., Secretary of the Entomological Society of London. Part I.—"On the Seasonal Dimorphism of Butterflies," containing Original Communications by Mr. W. H. EDWARDS, of Coalburgh. With two Coloured Plates. Price of Part I. (to Subscribers for the whole work only), 8*s* ; Part II. (6 coloured plates), 16*s*. ; Part III., 6*s*.

Sugar Beet (The). Including a History of the Beet Sugar Industry in Europe, Varieties of the Sugar Beet, Examination, Soils, Tillage, Seeds and Sowing, Yield and Cost of Cultivation, Harvesting, Transportation, Conservation, Feeding Qualities of the Beet and of the Pulp, &c. By L. S. WARE. Illustrated. 8vo, cloth extra, 21*s*.

Sullivan (A. M., M.P.). See "New Ireland."

Sulphuric Acid (A Practical Treatise on the Manufacture of). By A. G. and C. G. LOCK, Consulting Chemical Engineers. With 77 Construction Plates, and other Illustrations. Royal 8vo, 2*l.* 12*s. 6d.*

Sumner (Hon. Charles). See Life and Letters.

Sunrise: A Story of These Times. By WILLIAM BLACK, Author of "A Daughter of Heth," &c. 3 vols., 31*s. 6d.*

Surgeon's Handbook on the Treatment of Wounded in War. By Dr. FRIEDRICH ESMARCH, Professor of Surgery in the University of Kiel, and Surgeon-General to the Prussian Army. Translated by H. H. CLUTTON, B.A. Cantab, F.R.C.S. Numerous Coloured Plates and Illustrations, 8vo, strongly bound in flexible leather, 1*l.* 8*s.*

Sylvan Spring. By FRANCIS GEORGE HEATH. Illustrated by 12 Coloured Plates, drawn by F. E. HULME, F.L.S., Artist and Author of "Familiar Wild Flowers;" by 16 full-page, and more than 100 other Wood Engravings. Large post 8vo, cloth, gilt edges, 12*s. 6d.*

TAUCHNITZ'S English Editions of German Authors. Each volume, cloth flexible, 2*s*. ; or sewed, 1*s. 6d.* (Catalogues post free on application.)

—— (*B.*) *German and English Dictionary.* Cloth, 1*s. 6d.*; roan, 2*s*.

—— *French and English.* Paper, 1*s. 6d.* ; cloth, 2*s*. ; roan 2*s. 6d.*

Tauchnitz (B.) Italian and English Dictionary. Paper, 1s. 6d.; cloth, 2s.; roan, 2s. 6d.

———— *Spanish and English.* Paper, 1s. 6d.; cloth, 2s.; roan, 2s. 6d.

———— *New Testament.* Cloth, 2s.; gilt, 2s. 6d.

Taylor (Bayard). See "Studies in German Literature."

Through America; or, Nine Months in the United States. By W. G. MARSHALL, M.A. With nearly 100 Woodcuts of Views of Utah country and the famous Yosemite Valley; The Giant Trees, New York, Niagara, San Francisco, &c.; containing a full account of Mormon Life, as noted by the Author during his visits to Salt Lake City in 1878 and 1879. In 1 vol., demy 8vo, 21s.

Through the Dark Continent: The Sources of the Nile; Around the Great Lakes, and down the Congo. By HENRY M. STANLEY. 2 vols., demy 8vo, containing 150 Full-page and other Illustrations, 2 Portraits of the Author, and 10 Maps, 42s. Seventh Thousand. Cheaper Edition, crown 8vo, with some of the Illustrations and Maps. 1 vol., 12s. 6d.

Tour of the Prince of Wales in India. See RUSSELL.

Trees and Ferns. By F. G. HEATH. Crown 8vo, cloth, gilt edges, with numerous Illustrations, 3s. 6d.

Two Friends. By LUCIEN BIART, Author of "Adventures of a Young Naturalist," "My Rambles in the New World," &c. Small post 8vo, numerous Illustrations, gilt edges, 7s. 6d.; plainer binding, 5s.

Two Supercargoes (The); or, Adventures in Savage Africa. By W. H. G. KINGSTON. Numerous Full-page Illustrations. Square imperial 16mo, cloth extra, gilt edges, 7s. 6d.; plainer binding, 5s.

UNDER the Punkah. By PHIL ROBINSON, Author of "In my Indian Garden." Crown 8vo, limp cloth, uniform with the above, 3s. 6d.

Up and Down; or, Fifty Years' Experiences in Australia, California, New Zealand, India, China, and the South Pacific. Being the Life History of Capt. W. J. BARRY. Written by Himself. With several Illustrations. Crown 8vo, cloth extra, 8s. 6d.

BOOKS BY JULES VERNE.

Large Crown 8vo	Containing 350 to 600 pp. and from 50 to 100 full-page illustrations.		Containing the whole of the text with some illustrations.	
WORKS.	In very handsome cloth binding, gilt edges.	In plainer binding, plain edges.	In cloth binding, gilt edges, smaller type.	Coloured Boards.
	s. d.	s. d.	s. d.	
Twenty Thousand Leagues under the Sea. Part I. Ditto. Part II.	10 6	5 0	3 6	2 vols., 1s. each.
Hector Servadac . . .	10 6	5 0		
The Fur Country . . .	10 6	5 0	3 6	2 vols., 1s. each.
From the Earth to the Moon and a Trip round it	10 6	5 0	2 vols., 2s. each.	2 vols., 1s. each.
Michael Strogoff, the Courier of the Czar . .	10 6	5 0		
Dick Sands, the Boy Captain	10 6	5 0		s. d.
Five Weeks in a Balloon .	7 6	3 6	2 0	1 0
Adventures of Three Englishmen and Three Russians	7 6	3 6	2 0	1 0
Around the World in Eighty Days	7 6	3 6	2 0	1 0
A Floating City	7 6	3 6	2 0	1 0
The Blockade Runners .			2 0	1 0
Dr. Ox's Experiment . .			2 0	1 0
Master Zacharius . . .	7 6	3 6	2 0	1 0
A Drama in the Air . .				
A Winter amid the Ice .			2 0	1 0
The Survivors of the "Chancellor"	7 6	3 6	2 0	2 vols. 1s. each.
Martin Paz			2 0	1 0
THE MYSTERIOUS ISLAND, 3 vols. :—	22 6	10 6	6 0	3 0
Vol. I. Dropped from the Clouds	7 6	3 6	2 0	1 0
Vol. II. Abandoned . .	7 6	3 6	2 0	1 0
Vol. III. Secret of the Island	7 6	3 6	2 0	1 0
The Child of the Cavern .	7 6	3 6		
The Begum's Fortune . .	7 6			
The Tribulations of a Chinaman	7 6			
THE STEAM HOUSE, 2 vols.:—				
Vol. I. The Demon of Cawnpore	7 6			
Vol. II. Tigers and Traitors	7 6			

CELEBRATED TRAVELS AND TRAVELLERS. 3 vols. Demy 8vo, 600 pp., upwards of 100 full-page illustrations, 12s. 6d.; gilt edges, 14s. each :—
(1) THE EXPLORATION OF THE WORLD.
(2) THE GREAT NAVIGATORS OF THE EIGHTEENTH CENTURY.
(3) THE GREAT EXPLORERS OF THE NINETEENTH CENTURY.

WALLER (Rev. C. H.) The Names on the Gates of Pearl, and other Studies. By the Rev. C. H. WALLER, M.A. Second Edition. Crown 8vo, cloth extra, 6s.

———— *A Grammar and Analytical Vocabulary of the Words in* the Greek Testament. Compiled from Brüder's Concordance. For the use of Divinity Students and Greek Testament Classes. By the Rev. C. H. WALLER, M.A. Part I., The Grammar. Small post 8vo, cloth, 2s. 6d. Part II. The Vocabulary, 2s. 6d.

———— *Adoption and the Covenant.* Some Thoughts on Confirmation. Super-royal 16mo, cloth limp, 2s. 6d.

Warner (C. D.) My Summer in a Garden. Rose Library, 1s.

———— *Back-log Studies.* Boards, 1s. 6d.; cloth, 2s.

———— *In the Wilderness.* Rose Library, 1s.

———— *Mummies and Moslems.* 8vo, cloth, 12s.

Weaving. See "History and Principles."

Wills, A Few Hints on Proving, without Professional Assistance. By a PROBATE COURT OFFICIAL. 5th Edition, revised with Forms of Wills, Residuary Accounts, &c. Fcap. 8vo, cloth limp, 1s.

With Axe and Rifle on the Western Prairies. By W. H. G. KINGSTON. With numerous Illustrations, square crown 8vo, cloth extra, gilt edges, 7s. 6d.; plainer binding, 5s.

Woolsey (C. D., LL.D.) Introduction to the Study of Inter- national Law; designed as an Aid in Teaching and in Historical Studies. 5th Edition, demy 8vo, 18s.

Words of Wellington: Maxims and Opinions, Sentences and Reflections of the Great Duke, gathered from his Despatches, Letters, and Speeches (Bayard Series). 2s. 6d.

Wreck of the Grosvenor. By W. CLARK RUSSELL, Author of "John Holdsworth, Chief Mate," "A Sailor's Sweetheart," &c. 6s. Third and Cheaper Edition.

London:

SAMPSON LOW, MARSTON, SEARLE, & RIVINGTON,

CROWN BUILDINGS, 188, FLEET STREET, E.C.

CPSIA information can be obtained at www.ICGtesting.com
230883LV00004B/241/P